The Lying Kind

Anthony Neilson

Methuen Drama

Published by Methuen 2002

1 3 5 7 9 10 8 6 4 2

First published in 2002 by
Methuen Publishing Limited,
215 Vauxhall Bridge Road,
London SW1V 1EJ

Methuen Publishing Limited Reg. No. 3543167

A CIP catalogue record is available from the British Library

ISBN 0 413 77314 0

Typeset by SX Composing DTP, Rayleigh, Essex
Printed and bound in Great Britain by
Cox & Wyman Ltd, Reading, Berkshire

Caution

This text was correct before rehearsals began but does not include
changes which may have been made during rehearsal.

ROYAL COURT

Royal Court Theatre presents

THE LYING KIND

by **Anthony Neilson**

First performance at the Royal Court Jerwood Theatre Downstairs
Sloane Square, London on 23 November 2002.

Supported by the Royal Court's PRODUCTION SYNDICATE scheme

THE LYING KIND

by **Anthony Neilson**

Cast in order of appearance

Gobbel **Thomas Fisher**
Blunt **Darrell D'Silva**
Gronya **Alison Newman**
Garson **Sheila Burrell**
Balthasar **Patrick Godfrey**
Reverend Shandy **Matthew Pidgeon**
Carol **Kellie Shirley**

Director **Anthony Neilson**
Designer **Bob Bailey**
Lighting Designer **Chahine Yavroyan**
Sound Designer **Neil Alexander**
Assistant Director **Jennie Fellows**
Casting Director **Lisa Makin**
Production Manager **Paul Handley**
Stage Manager **Tariq Rifaat**
Deputy Stage Manager **Caroline Healey**
Assistant Stage Manager **Nicole Keighly**
Costume Supervisor **Iona Kenrick**
Company Voice Work **Patsy Rodenburg**
Set built by **Bower Wood Production Services**
Painted by **Richard Nutbourne**

Royal Court Theatre would like to thank the following for their help with this production:
Wardrobe care by Persil and Comfort courtesy of Lever Fabergé.

THE COMPANY

Anthony Neilson (writer and director)
At the Royal Court plays written and directed
include: The Censor (The Red Room at the
Finborough), Penetrator (Traverse).
Other theatre includes: Stitching (The Red Room at
the Traverse/Bush); Edward Gant's Amazing Feats
of Loneliness (The Drum, Plymouth); The Night
Before Christmas (The Red Room); The Year of the
Family (Finborough); Normal (Edinburgh Festival).
Films include: The Debt Collector, Deeper Still.
Awards include: Writers' Guild Award 1997 for Best
Fringe Play, Time Out Live Award 1997 for The
Censor, shortlisted for the Evening Standard award
for Most Promising Playwright 2002 for Stitching,
Anthony has also written for radio.

Neil Alexander (sound designer)
For the Royal Court: Moving On, Let's all Go to the
Fair, The Rough Ride to Survival, Clubbed Out,
Love Risk, Don't Blame Her, Back to Back, Yard
Gal, Been So Long, Fair Game, Bailegangaire,
Heredity.
Other theatre includes: She Stoops To Conquer/A
Laughing Matter (Out of Joint/RNT); The
Threepenny Opera, Prayer for Owen Meany, Life
after Life, Vincent in Brixton, The Chain Play,
Mother Clap's Molly House, International
Connections, Marriage Play/Finding the Sun,
Remembrance of Things Past, The Waiting Room,
Blue Orange, Sparkleshark (RNT); Observe the
Sons of Ulster Marching Towards the Somme
(Pleasance); Two Horsemen (Gate/Bush); The
Snake House (Greenwich); Shuffling Off, Northern
Lights (New Grove); The Year of the Family
(Finborough); Penetrator
(Traverse/Finborough/RCT).
Film includes: Private Dancer & Dog Fight.

Bob Bailey (designer)
Theatre includes: Stitching (The Red Room at the
Traverse/Bush); Tosca (Nationale Reisopera,
Holland); The Happiest Days of My Life (DV8
Dance Company, UK and European tour); Edward
Gant's Amazing Feats of Loneliness (The Drum,
Plymouth); Aeroplane Man (Stratford East); La
Ronde (RADA); Grapes of Wrath (Finborough);
Angels in America (Crucible, Sheffield); Blueprint
(Royal Opera House Education); Venezia (RNT
Studio/Gate); Hijrah (The Drum, Plymouth/Bush);
Charley's Aunt (Crucible, Sheffield); Dancing at
Lughnasa (Jermyn Street); Mrs Harris Goes to Paris
(London's Children's Ballet, Peacock); Horseplay, All
Nighter (Royal Ballet); Good Works, Rough Music
(Show of Strength, Bristol).
Awards include: 1999 Time Out Designer of the
Year Award for The Happiest Days of My Life.

Sheila Burrell
For the Royal Court: Last Dance at Dum
Dum (Ambassadors), Salonika, West of Suez.
Other theatre includes: Phaedra (Riverside);
Finding the Sun, Absolute Hell, Macbeth,
School for Scandal (RNT); The Handy Man
(Minerva Theatre, Chichester); Little Eyolf
(Orange Tree); Great Expectations (Ashcroft,
Old Vic); Strange Interlude (Duke of York);
My Fair Lady (for Simon Callow); The
Bacchae (Actors Company); King John,
Richard I I I (RSC); A Severed Head
(Criterion); Dark of the Moon (Ambassadors).
Film includes: The Woodlanders (River Films),
Jane Eyre (Zeferelli), Afraid of the Dark.
Television includes: William and Mary (LWT),
Always & Everyone (Granada), Perfect
Strangers (Talkback Productions), Trial and
Retribution I I I (Lynda La Plante
Productions), Casualty, Hetty Wainthrop
Investigates, The Bill, Cold Comfort Farm
(Thames), Heartbeat (YTV), Bramwell
(Carlton), Darling Buds of May (ITV), Devices
and Desires, Gaudy Night, Trial of Klaus
Barbie, The Tribute, Frost in May, The Six
Wives of Henry VI I I.

Darrell D'Silva
Theatre includes: A Midsummer Night's
Dream (RSC & international tour); Antarctica
(Northern Party Ltd); Six Characters Looking
for An Author (Young Vic); Further than the
Furthest Thing (Tron, Glasgow/RNT); Tear
from a Glass Eye (Gate); Closer (RNT tour);
A Month in the Country, Troilus & Cressida,
Camino Real, Spanish Tragedy, Henry VI I I,
Dr Faustus (RSC); Chasing the Moment (One
Tree Theatre Company); Romeo & Juliet, The
Three Muskeeters (Crucible, Sheffield);
Crossfire (Paines Plough).
Film includes: Dirty Pretty Things (BBC).
Television includes: Cambridge Spies, Out of
the Blue (BBC), Dinotopia (Thistle
Management Ltd), Table Twelve: After Hours
(World Productions), The Bill (Thames),
Queen of Swords: The Dragon (Amy
International Artists), In Defence, Prime
Suspect (Granada), Wokenwell (LWT), Faith
(Central Films).
Radio includes: A Suit of Lights (BBC Radio),
Cry Wolf (BBC Radio 4), A Game of Three
Halves (BBC Radio, Cardiff).

Jennie Fellows (assistant director)
As director, theatre includes: The Wake (Soho
Theatre Studio); Tight Rope Walking (Cockpit).
As assistant director, theatre includes: Trip's
Cinch (Southwark Playhouse);
oneminutesilence (ATC at the Young Vic);
Penthisilea (New End).
Jennie is also a script reader for the Royal Court
Young Writers' Programme.

Thomas Fisher
For the Royal Court: The Glory of Living.
Other theatre includes: The Comedy of Errors
(RSC); Resolution (BAC); The Angel and the
Bouncer (Edinburgh Fringe); Hansel & Gretel,
Mirandolina (Lyric Hammersmith); 50
Revolutions (Whitehall); Leonce & Lena, The
Lovers, The Great Highway (Gate).
Film includes: Shanghai Knights (Spyglass
Entertainment), Club Le Monde (Screen
Productions), The Mummy Returns
(Universal/Alphaville), Enigma (Jagged Films), The
Truth Game (Screen Productions), The Nine
Lives of Thomas Katz (Strawberry Vale), Simon
Magus (Silesia Films Ltd).
Television includes: Casualty (BBC), North
Square (Company Television), Active Defence
(Granada).
Awards include: winner of Best Actor at Porto
Film Festival for The Nine Lives of Thomas Katz.

Patrick Godfrey
For the Royal Court: Life Price, Inside Out.
Other theatre includes: The Lady's Not for
Burning (Minerva Theatre, Chichester); Battle
Royal, Mary Stuart (RNT); The Iceman Cometh
(Almeida Theatre, Old Vic, Broadway); The
Winter's Tale, The Maid's Tragedy (Globe); The
Importance of Being Earnest (Birmingham
Repertory/Old Vic); Agamemnon's Children,
Walpurgis Night (Gate); Galileo (Almeida);
Phoenix (Bush); Uncle Vanya (Renaissance tour);
Barbarians, Romeo and Juliet, Hamlet (RSC);
Nicholas Nickelby, Summerfolk, Love's Labours
Lost (Aldwych/New York); Section Nine,
Macbeth, Merry Wives, Cymbeline, Baal,
(Stratford); Devil's Disciple (Aldwych); Twelfth
Night (RSC tour); Bewitched
(Stratford/Aldwych); The Three Sisters
(Stratford/Tour); The Cherry Orchard (Crucible,
Sheffield); Wildoats (Aldwych/Globe); Too True
to be Good (Aldwych/Piccadilly); Saints Day (St
Martins); School for Scandal (Haymarket).
Film includes: The Importance of Being Earnest
(Fragile Films), The Count of Monte Cristo
(Chateau D'If), My Brother Tom (MBT
Productions), Ever After (20th Century Fox),

Remains of the Day, Maurice, Heat and Dust, A
Room with a View (Merchant Ivory), The Trial
(BBC Films), On the Black Hill (BFI), Nicholas
Nickleby (Primetime).
Television includes: Heartbeat, Medics (Granada),
Foyle's War (Greenlit Productions), The
Falklands Play, Lives of Animals (BBC 4),
Doctors, Casualty, The Beast in Man, Landing on
the Sun, You Me and It, Redemption, Shadow of
the Noose, Pulaski, A Perfect Spy, The
Interrogation of John, The Devil's Disciple, Miss
Marple's Nemesis, Pericles, Cyrano de Bergerac,
The Possessed, (BBC), Midsomer Murders
(Bentley Productions), Hearts and Bones
(United), Kavanagh (Carlton), Bramwell, A
Dance to the Music of Time, Behaving Badly, The
New Statesman (YTV), The Bill, The Three
Sisters (Thames), Shades (Meridian), Branwell
(Carlton), Dandelion Dead (LWT), Inspector
Morse (Zenith), Sherlock Holmes (Anglia), My
Friend Walter (Portobello Productions), Do Not
Disturb (BBC Screen Two), Come Home Charlie
and Face Them, The Charmer (LWT), Poirot
(ITV), Auf Wiedersehn Pet (Central), Antony and
Cleopatra (ATV).

Alison Newman
For the Royal Court: The Censor (The Red
Room at the Finborough).
Theatre includes: Night of the Soul, Luminosity,
Loveplay (RSC Pit); Smile, The Games Room
(Soho); The Tempest (Royal Exchange).
Film includes: Ashes & Sand (Open Road Films).
Television includes: Footballers' Wives 1 & 2
(Shed for ITV), The Prince and the Pauper
(Hallmark), Bad Girls (Shed for ITV), The Bill
(Thames), Touching Evil III (United
Productions), Great Expectations (BBC),
Butterfly Collectors (Granada).

Matthew Pidgeon
Theatre includes: Edward Gant's Amazing Feats
of Loneliness (Theatre Royal, Plymouth);
Antigone, The Phoenix, The Grapes of Wrath,
Born Guilty (7.84); The Sex Comedies
(Watermans Arts Centre & Edinburgh Fringe),
Twelfth Night (Salisbury Playhouse); Caucasian
Chalk Circle, Hamlet, Montrose, The Glass
Menagerie, Romeo & Juliet (Royal Lyceum,
Edinburgh); Dave's Last Laugh (Tron, Glasgow);
Playing Hide & Seek with Jesus (Pleasance,
Edinburgh).
Film includes: The Winslow Boy, A Shot at Glory,
State & Main.
Television includes: Rockface (Union
Pictures/BBC), Taggart (STV), This Morning with
Richard not Judy, Casualty (BBC).

Kellie Shirley
Theatre includes: X Generation (Lewisham
Theatre); Chasing Dolphins (Churchill Theatre);
West Side Story (Royal Albert Hall).
Film includes: Whacked (Halyon Films), Flush
(Freehand Productions), Sticky (Aurora
Productions).
Television includes: Jekyll & Hyde (Working
Title), Small Pox 2002 Silent Weapon (BBC/Wall
to Wall).

Chahine Yavroyan (lighting designer)
For the Royal Court: Outlying Islands (Traverse).
Other theatre includes: Stitching (The Red Room
at the Traverse/Bush Theatre); Edward Gant's
Amazing Feats of Loneliness (The Drum,
Plymouth); Whistlestop, Shang-a-Lang, Darwin's
Flood (Bush); Green Field, Gagarin Way, King of
the Fields, The Speculator, Perfect Days, Anna
Weiss, Knives in Hens, The Architect (Traverse);
South Pacific, King Lear (Crucible, Sheffield);
Pygmalion (Nottingham Playhouse); A
Midsummer Night's Dream, Macbeth
(Haymarket, Leicester); Hedda Gabler, Wolk's
World (Royal Exchange); Standing Room Only,
Tantamount Esperance (Rose English, 1st Class
Evening's Entertainment for Post Operative
Productions).

THE ENGLISH STAGE COMPANY AT THE ROYAL COURT

The English Stage Company at the Royal Court opened in 1956 as a subsidised theatre producing new British plays, international plays and some classical revivals.

The first artistic director George Devine aimed to create a writers' theatre, 'a place where the dramatist is acknowledged as the fundamental creative force in the theatre and where the play is more important than the actors, the director, the designer'. The urgent need was to find a contemporary style in which the play, the acting, direction and design are all combined. He believed that 'the battle will be a long one to continue to create the right conditions for writers to work in'.

Devine aimed to discover 'hard-hitting, uncompromising writers whose plays are stimulating, provocative and exciting'. The Royal Court production of John Osborne's Look Back in Anger in May 1956 is now seen as the decisive starting point of modern British drama and the policy created a new generation of British playwrights. The first wave included John Osborne, Arnold Wesker, John Arden, Ann Jellicoe, N F Simpson and Edward Bond. Early seasons included new international plays by Bertolt Brecht, Eugène Ionesco, Samuel Beckett, Jean-Paul Sartre and Marguerite Duras.

The theatre started with the 400-seat proscenium arch Theatre Downstairs, and then in 1969 opened a second theatre, the 60-seat studio Theatre Upstairs. Some productions transfer to the West End, such as Caryl Churchill's Far Away, Conor McPherson's The Weir, Kevin Elyot's Mouth to Mouth and My Night With Reg. The Royal Court also co-produces plays which have transferred to the West End or toured internationally, such as Sebastian Barry's The Steward of Christendom and Mark Ravenhill's Shopping and Fucking (with Out of Joint), Martin McDonagh's The Beauty Queen Of Leenane (with Druid Theatre Company), Ayub Khan-Din's East is East (with Tamasha Theatre Company, and now a feature film).

Since 1994 the Royal Court's artistic policy has again been vigorously directed to finding and producing a new generation of playwrights. The writers include Joe Penhall, Rebecca Prichard, Michael Wynne, Nick Grosso, Judy Upton, Meredith Oakes, Sarah Kane, Anthony Neilson, Judith Johnson, James Stock, Jez Butterworth, Marina Carr, Phyllis Nagy, Simon Block, Martin McDonagh, Mark Ravenhill, Ayub Khan-Din, Tamantha Hammerschlag, Jess Walters, Che Walker, Conor McPherson, Simon Stephens,

photo: Andy Chopping

Richard Bean, Roy Williams, Gary Mitchell, Mick Mahoney, Rebecca Gilman, Christopher Shinn, Kia Corthron, David Gieselmann, Marius von Mayenburg, David Eldridge, Leo Butler, Zinnie Harris, Grae Cleugh, Roland Schimmelpfennig and Vassily Sigarev. This expanded programme of new plays has been made possible through the support of A.S.K Theater Projects, the Jerwood Charitable Foundation, the American Friends of the Royal Court Theatre and many in association with the Royal National Theatre Studio.

In recent years there have been record-breaking productions at the box office, with capacity houses for Caryl Churchill's A Number, Jez Butterworth's The Night Heron, Rebecca Gilman's Boy Gets Girl, Kevin Elyot's Mouth To Mouth, David Hare's My Zinc Bed and Conor McPherson's The Weir, which transferred to the West End in October 1998 and ran for nearly two years at the Duke of York's Theatre.

The newly refurbished theatre in Sloane Square opened in February 2000, with a policy still inspired by the first artistic director George Devine. The Royal Court is an international theatre for new plays and new playwrights, and the work shapes contemporary drama in Britain and overseas.

Funded by
THE
ARTS
COUNCIL
OF ENGLAND

PROGRAMME SUPPORTERS

The Royal Court (English Stage Company Ltd) receives its principal funding from London Arts. It is also supported financially by a wide range of private companies and public bodies and earns the remainder of its income from the box office and its own trading activities.
The Royal Borough of Kensington & Chelsea gives an annual grant to the Royal Court Young Writers' Programme and the Affiliation of London Government provides project funding for a number of play development initiatives.

The Jerwood Charitable Foundation continues to support new plays by new playwrights through the Jerwood New Playwrights series. Since 1993 the A.S.K. Theater Projects of Los Angeles has funded a Playwrights' Programme at the theatre. Bloomberg Mondays, the Royal Court's reduced price ticket scheme, is supported by Bloomberg. Over the past seven years the BBC has supported the Gerald Chapman Fund for directors.

London Government   LONDON ARTS

AWARDS FOR
THE ROYAL COURT

Terry Johnson's Hysteria won the 1994 Olivier Award for Best Comedy, and also the Writers' Guild Award for Best West End Play. Kevin Elyot's My Night with Reg won the 1994 Writers' Guild Award for Best Fringe Play, the Evening Standard Award for Best Comedy, and the 1994 Olivier Award for Best Comedy. Joe Penhall was joint winner of the 1994 John Whiting Award for Some Voices. Sebastian Barry won the 1995 Writers' Guild Award for Best Fringe Play, the Critics' Circle Award and the 1995 Lloyds Private Banking Playwright of the Year Award for The Steward of Christendom. Jez Butterworth won the 1995 George Devine Award, the Writers' Guild New Writer of the Year Award, the Evening Standard Award for Most Promising Playwright and the Olivier Award for Best Comedy for Mojo.

The Royal Court was the overall winner of the 1995 Prudential Award for the Arts for creativity, excellence, innovation and accessibility. The Royal Court Theatre Upstairs won the 1995 Peter Brook Empty Space Award for innovation and excellence in theatre.

Michael Wynne won the 1996 Meyer-Whitworth Award for The Knocky. Martin McDonagh won the 1996 George Devine Award, the 1996 Writers' Guild Best Fringe Play Award, the 1996 Critics' Circle Award and the 1996 Evening Standard Award for Most Promising Playwright for The Beauty Queen of Leenane. Marina Carr won the 19th Susan Smith Blackburn Prize (1996/7) for Portia Coughlan. Conor McPherson won the 1997 George Devine Award, the 1997 Critics' Circle Award and the 1997 Evening Standard Award for Most Promising Playwright for The Weir. Ayub Khan-Din won the 1997 Writers' Guild Awards for Best West End Play and Writers' Guild New Writer of the Year and the 1996 John Whiting Award for East is East (co-production with Tamasha).

At the 1998 Tony Awards, Martin McDonagh's The Beauty Queen of Leenane (co-production with Druid Theatre Company) won four awards including Garry Hynes for Best Director and was nominated for a further two. Eugene Ionesco's The Chairs (co-production with Theatre de Complicite) was nominated for six Tony awards. David Hare won the 1998 Time Out Live Award for Outstanding Achievement and six awards in New York including the Drama League, Drama Desk and New York Critics Circle Award for Via Dolorosa. Sarah Kane won the 1998 Arts Foundation Fellowship in Playwriting. Rebecca Prichard won the 1998 Critics' Circle Award for Most Promising Playwright for Yard Gal (co-production with Clean Break).

Conor McPherson won the 1999 Olivier Award for Best New Play for The Weir. The Royal Court won the 1999 ITI Award for Excellence in International Theatre. Sarah Kane's Cleansed was judged Best Foreign Language Play in 1999 by Theater Heute in Germany. Gary Mitchell won the 1999 Pearson Best Play Award for Trust. Rebecca Gilman was joint winner of the 1999 George Devine Award and won the 1999 Evening Standard Award for Most Promising Playwright for The Glory of Living.

In 1999, the Royal Court won the European theatre prize New Theatrical Realities, presented at Taormina Arte in Sicily, for its efforts in recent years in discovering and producing the work of young British dramatists.

Roy Williams and Gary Mitchell were joint winners of the George Devine Award 2000 for Most Promising Playwright for Lift Off and The Force of Change respectively. At the Barclays Theatre Awards 2000 presented by the TMA, Richard Wilson won the Best Director Award for David Gieselmann's Mr Kolpert and Jeremy Herbert won the Best Designer Award for Sarah Kane's 4.48 Psychosis. Gary Mitchell won the Evening Standard's Charles Wintour Award 2000 for Most Promising Playwright for The Force of Change. Stephen Jeffreys' I Just Stopped by to See The Man won an AT&T: On Stage Award 2000. David Eldridge's Under the Blue Sky won the Time Out Live Award 2001 for Best New Play in the West End. Leo Butler won the George Devine Award 2001 for Most Promising Playwright for Redundant. Roy Williams won the Evening Standard's Charles Wintour Award 2001 for Most Promising Playwright for Clubland. Grae Cleugh won the 2001 Olivier Award for Most Promising Playwright for Fucking Games.

ROYAL COURT BOOKSHOP

The bookshop offers a wide range of playtexts and theatre books, with over 1,000 titles. Located in the downstairs Bar and Food area, the bookshop is open Monday to Saturday, afternoons and evenings.

Many Royal Court playtexts are available for just £2 including works by Harold Pinter, Caryl Churchill, Rebecca Gilman, Martin Crimp, Sarah Kane, Conor McPherson, Ayub Khan-Din, Timberlake Wertenbaker and Roy Williams.

For information on titles and special events, Email: bookshop@royalcourttheatre.com
Tel: 020 7565 5024

ROYAL COURT
BLOOMBERG MONDAYS

Visit www.bloombergmondays.com and write your own first scene of THE LYING KIND in the Royal Court's online scriptwriter - then add your own action...

ROYAL COURT
scriptwriter
www.bloombergmondays.com

**Bloomberg Mondays
ALL SEATS £7.50**

Available in advance for the Jerwood Theatre Downstairs and available from 10am on the day in person, at the Box Office (2 tickets per person) for the Jerwood Theatre Upstairs.

BOX OFFICE 020 7565 5000
BOOK ONLINE at
www.bloombergmondays.com

BLOOMERG have supported Monday nights at the Royal Court since 1998. This has enabled thousands of people to see Royal Court productions every Monday night for a reduced price in the best seats in the Jerwood Theatre Downstairs as well as in the Jerwood Theatre Upstairs.

Bloomberg

The Lying Kind

The Lying Kind premiered at the Royal Court Theatre, London, on 23 November, 2002. The cast was as follows:

Gobbel	Thomas Fisher
Blunt	Darrell D'Silva
Gronya	Alison Newman
Garson	Sheila Burrell
Balthasar	Patrick Godfrey
Reverend Shandy	Matthew Pidgeon
Carol	Kellie Shirley

Director Anthony Neilson
Designer Bob Bailey
Lighting Designer Chahine Yavroyan
Sound Designer Neil Alexander

Act One

A residential street. Iced with snow.

A main door – number 58. A sprig of plastic holly pinned to it. To one side of the door, a window – in which a small artificial tree glows with Christmas lights. Behind it, the room is dark.

In the distance, we can hear a group of people chanting something indistinct. It sounds aggressive.

The chanting passes away.

Enter **Blunt** *and* **Gobbel**, *two police constables.*

Gobbel   Did you hear that?

Blunt *is holding a piece of paper, checking for the door number.*

Blunt   This is it – number 58.

Blunt *tries to see into the house.*

Gobbel   People shouting something. Did you hear it?

Blunt   Never mind that. Let's get this over with.

Pause.

Blunt *nods at the door.*

Pause.

Gobbel   What?

Blunt   Ring the bell.

Gobbel   Me?

Blunt   Of course you.

Gobbel   Why me?

Blunt   Because you lost the toss.

Gobbel   To *tell* them – Not to ring the *bell*. Nothing about ringing the *bell* – !

Blunt   It's part and parcel.

Gobbel   Eh?

Blunt   If you don't ring the bell, they won't know we're here. And if they don't know we're here, you can't tell them, now, can you? Part And Parcel.

Pause.

Gobbel   Can't you ring it?

Blunt   I could. But it would set a dangerous precedent.

Gobbel   Would it?

Blunt   Certainly it would. If you say you're going to do something, I have to know you'll honour that to the letter. Remember what the sarge said – Can't trust your wife, you end up divorced. Can't trust your partner – you may well end up dead.

Gobbel   What, from ringing a doorbell?

Blunt   Today it's a doorbell. Tomorrow it's a madman with an axe and a sawn-off shotgun.

Pause.

Gobbel   We're not working tomorrow.

Blunt   I don't mean it literally.

Gobbel   Tomorrow's Christmas Day.

Blunt   I know that. (*Pause.*) Just go ahead and ring the bell.

Gobbel *nervously approaches the bell. He hesitates.*

Gobbel   How old are they?

Blunt   Who?

Pause. **Gobbel** *nods at the house.*

The parents?

Gobbel *nods.*

Blunt   How should I know?

Gobbel   Well, how old's the . . . ?

He nods at the house again.

Blunt   Deceased.

Gobbel   How old is she?

*Sighing, **Blunt** gets the scrap of paper out of his pocket.*

Blunt   Thirty-four.

Gobbel   Thirty-*four*?!

Blunt   What *about* it?

Gobbel   Well – if she's thirty-four – that means they must be . . .

Blunt   What?

Gobbel   *Old*!

*A momentary flicker betrays **Blunt**'s concern. Pause.*

Blunt   Not necessarily.

Gobbel   Thirty-four!?

Blunt   Maybe they had her at sixteen.

Gobbel   Sixteen?!!

Blunt   People have children at sixteen.

Gobbel   Not these days . . .

Blunt   But we're not talking about these days though, are we? We're talking about thirty-four years ago.

Pause.

Gobbel   Thirty-four plus sixteen . . .

Blunt   Fifty.

Gobbel   That's old!

Blunt   No it's not!

Gobbel   Fifty's old –

Blunt   Not these days it's not.

Gobbel   I thought we weren't *talking* about these days!

Blunt   Well, we are *now* . . .

Gobbel   Eh?

Blunt   We're talking about these days *now* –

Gobbel *wrestles with this.*

Blunt   Look – All I'm *saying* is that fifty isn't what it was. Fifty's just middle-aged now. Fifty – is what forty was, ten years ago.

Gobbel (*pause*)   What, thirty?

Blunt   What's the matter with you?! Their daughter's been killed on the motorway – !

Gobbel   *Sssshhh!!*

Blunt   Well, it's not an easy thing to hear at *any* age, is it?!

Gobbel   No, but – I mean – at least if they were young . . .

Pause.

Blunt   What?

Gobbel   Eh?

Blunt   At-least-if-they-were-young *what*?

Gobbel   Well – they'd still . . . have their whole lives . . . ahead of them.

Pause.

Blunt   You just open your mouth, don't you? You open your mouth and meaningless words just tumble out, like brain-damaged skydivers.
Now go ahead and ring the bell!

Again, **Gobbel** *contemplates. Again, he hesitates.*

Gobbel   The bell.

Blunt *nods.*

Gobbel   Not the knocker?

Blunt   No, the *bell.*

Gobbel (*nods*)   Right.

Pause.

Gobbel   Why not the knocker?

Blunt   Why not the *bell?*

Gobbel   Well, it might . . . give them a fright.

Blunt (*pause*)   Well, then use the *knocker* then!

Gobbel   D'you reckon?

Blunt   Whatever you *like!*

Gobbel   Right.

He rubs his cold hands together and approaches the bell.

You ready?

Blunt *nods, tensing himself.*

The holly takes **Gobbel**'s *interest.*

Blunt *watches as he inspects it.*

Gobbel   This holly's a bit loose . . .

Pause.

I'll just use the bell.

Blunt *sighs heavily.*

Gobbel   Ready?

Blunt   Stop asking me if I'm ready! Just ring the blood thing!

Again, **Gobbel** *rubs his hands and approaches the door. Again,* **Blunt** *tenses.*

Yet again, **Gobbel** *hesitates.*

Blunt   What is it *now*?!

Gobbel   I'm scared!

Blunt   Oh, don't be ridiculous!

Gobbel   You're not scared?

Blunt   What's there to be scared of?

Gobbel   Because they might be old and frail and hearing this – it could *kill* them. Blunt! The shock could kill them stone *dead*!

Blunt   Don't talk rubbish!

Gobbel   You do it then! If I'm talking rubbish, you do it!

Blunt   I did the last one!

Gobbel   So you're more experienced!

Blunt   I don't *want* to be more experienced! I want to be *less* experienced!

Gobbel   You can't be *less* experienced!

Blunt   I can be less experienced than I'll be if I have to experience it *again*!

Gobbel   Yes, but not yet!

Blunt (*pause*)   *You* – are going to ring that bell – if I have to use your severed hand to do it!

Gobbel *is a little shocked by* **Blunt***'s ferocity.*

Gobbel   There's no reason to be like that.

Blunt   There's a hundred reasons and they're all you!

Pause.

Gobbel   There's no need to be nasty about it.

Blunt   I'm not 'being' – ! (*Pause.*) Look – I'm no happier about this than you. But being a policeman can't be just moving on buskers or exchanging friendly banter with the Countryside Alliance. There's bound to be some bad bits too. We knew that when we joined.

Pause.

Think of it this way: it's Christmas Eve. We just have to do this one thing and then that's us, for two whole days. Think about that. Two whole days of getting up whenever the fancy takes us. No trudging around all day in stiff new shoes. We'll get the fire going –

Gobbel   Both bars?

Blunt   Both bars, why not? And we'll sit there with our feet up, sipping warm brandy from the fancy glasses; paper hats, Eric and Ernie and the friendly smell of slowly roasting turkey . . .

Pause. **Blunt** *gets lost in his own reverie.*

Gobbel   Blunt?

Blunt   Mmm?

Gobbel   I couldn't get a turkey.

Blunt   Why not?

Gobbel   They didn't have any left.

Blunt   So what did you get?

Pause.

Gobbel   Dutch sausage.

Pause.

Blunt   Dutch sausage.

Gobbel   You know, the ones like that – (*He makes a horseshoe shape.*) Like a magnet. In a bag and you / boil them.

Blunt   I know what it is.

Gobbel   They're not as Christmassy as turkey but they're a lot quicker to cook.

Pause.

They're nice with beans.

Blunt   Well, we can discuss that *later*. What I'm saying is that we have to look beyond the task at hand; not at the stormy seas around us but at the calm horizon ahead. You see?

Gobbel   The calm horizon ahead.

Blunt   Exactly.

Gobbel (*nods*)   Not the stormy seas around us . . .

Blunt   The calm horizon ahead.

Gobbel (*nods*)   Right.

Blunt   Got it?

Gobbel   Yes.

Suddenly, **Gobbel** *reaches out to press the bell – this time, it's* **Blunt** *that stops him.*

Blunt   What are you doing?!

Gobbel   I'm ringing the bell!?

Blunt   You didn't ask if I was ready!

Gobbel   I thought you told me not to!?

Blunt   I didn't expect you to listen!

Pause. **Gobbel** *points at him.*

Gobbel   You *are* scared!

Blunt   Nonsense!

Gobbel   You are! You're just as scared as I am, and you're right because it's terrible! Because it's Christmas Eve and they're in there all warm and nice with the holly and the tree and no idea that any minute now it's all going to be ruined! Their lives are going to be ruined and it's us that's going to ruin them!

Blunt   Stop saying that!

Gobbel   I thought we were going to help people, not ruin their lives!

Blunt   It's not our fault what's happened!

Gobbel   It'll be our fault they know about it!

Blunt   Well, someone's got to tell them!

Gobbel   Do they? Why? Maybe they don't want to know! Who are we to go telling people things?!

Blunt   You're talking rubbish!

Gobbel   Am I? Everybody doesn't have to know everything, you know! Haven't you ever been happy not knowing something?

Blunt   What are you talking about?

Gobbel   It's true though, isn't it?

Blunt   It's nonsense! How would I know if I was happy not knowing something unless I knew what it was I didn't know?!

Gobbel   No, because you said – you *told* me – when Racquel went off with that man on your honeymoon –

Blunt   That was completely different –

Gobbel   You told me; you wished you hadn't found out!

Blunt   Found *them*! I wished I hadn't found *them*!

Gobbel   Because you were happy not knowing!

Blunt   Yes, but I don't look back on it and think, 'Wasn't it awful my bride betraying me with a hot-dog seller but oh well, at least I had a nice holiday in Tenerife,' do I?!

Gobbel   Don't you?!

Blunt   No, I *don't!* All I feel is twice the idiot. Once because my wife was betraying me and twice cos all the time it was happening, I was wandering round town in a massive sombrero!

Pause.

Gobbel   A sombrero.

Blunt *nods, ruefully.*

Gobbel   I didn't know.

Blunt   Fine if you never find out. But you do. And so will they. All you're doing is delaying the inevitable.

Gobbel   Good! It's always rotten anyway!

Blunt *notices someone standing offstage.*

Gobbel   Why can't good things be inevitable? Why can't being happy or rich be inevitable? But they're not. It's just rotten things like dying and getting ill –

Blunt *pats him quiet.* **Gobbel** *turns to see what he is seeing.*

Pause.

Blunt   May we be of any assistance at all?

Pause. And then a huge person enters – a brick shithouse, complete with blue-ink graffiti and the face you only get from a hard, hard life. This is **Gronya***.*

As she approaches, **Gobbel** *edges behind* **Blunt***. She takes a while to look them up and down, dragging on her cigar.*

Gronya   Seen any people?

Pause.

Blunt   People?

Gobbel   People . . .

Blunt   Could you perhaps be a little more . . . specific?

Gronya   A *bunch* of people.

Pause.

Blunt   A bunch of people.

Gobbel   A bunch of people . . .

Gronya   A bunch of people with signs. Chanting stuff.

Gobbel   That's what I heard, remember? People chanting something –

Blunt   We heard them, but we didn't actually see them.

Gobbel   It was coming from over there.

Gronya   Over there?

Blunt   Yes – over that way, somewhere.

She doesn't move. Pause. **Blunt** *and* **Gobbel** *shift nervously.*

Gobbel   Why's she staring at us like that?

Blunt   I don't know.
Is there a problem at all?

Gronya   You tell me.

Pause.

Blunt   I don't *think* so . . .

Gronya   So why're you here?

Blunt   We're here on a police matter.

Gronya   Is that right? And what would that be then?

Blunt   I'm afraid we're not at liberty to divulge that.

Gronya   Not at liberty.

Gobbel   That means we can't tell you.

Gronya   Are you trying to be funny?

Gobbel   No, sir.

Blunt *elbows* **Gobbel**.

Blunt   Excuse my colleague. He also has difficulty with left and right. But – in answer to your question – no: we are not attempting to be humorous.

Gronya   Just it's a funny thing to say; At Liberty. Makes me think it must be in your mind. Makes me think maybe someone *is* at liberty. Now who would that be?

Pause.

Gobbel   What's she on about?

Blunt   I don't know.

Gronya   You don't know. Well, maybe *this* – will refresh your memory.

Facing them, she opens her jacket, flasher-style. They stare at her chest.

Gobbel   PAPS?

Gronya   You what?

Gobbel   That's what it says!

She's wearing a T-shirt that does indeed say 'PAPS'.

Gronya   That's PARENTS AGAINST PAEDOPHILE SCUM. Ring any bells?

Blunt   Weren't you the ones that set fire to the shoeshop?

Gronya   That's never been proved, but yes – that's us. We're a small but highly organised group of local parents that has come together to combat the threat of paedophile scum being in the area and potentially buggering or otherwise touching up our kids.

Blunt   Well, that's all very well, miss, but –

Gronya   That's *Mrs.*

Blunt (*pause*)   Mrs. (*Pause.*) But – with respect – I'm afraid I fail to see the immediate relevance.

Gronya   Oh, you 'fail to see the immediate relevance', do you? Well – it just so happens that today we got a tip from a very reliable source that there happens to be such a dirty child-molesting bastard living in this actual vicinity. And that furthermore, this fact is known by you – the Dibble – and has been for quite some time. So what do you say to that?

Blunt   We don't know anything about it.

Gobbel *shakes his head.*

Blunt   But then we wouldn't; there's a special unit deals with all that.

Gronya (*nods*)   Is that so.
Cos then we got *another* tip. Said the coppers know that we know, and that they're going to smuggle the dirty nonce bastard out of town before we can get to him and administer the punishment he so richly deserves. (*Pause.*) I suppose you wouldn't know anything about that either?

Gobbel   Well, you suppose *wrong*.

Blunt   Right.

Gobbel   Right?

Blunt   She supposes *right*. We don't.

Gronya   Well, that's lucky for you. Cos if there's anything I hate *worse* – than a dirty, stinking paedophile – it's the dirty, stinking *traitors* that protect them. Wouldn't you agree?

They are non-committal. **Gronya** *approaches them, menacingly.*

After all, a paedo's sick, like a rabid dog. He can't help himself. All you can do with a paedo is just –

She makes a sudden gesture and sound, like snapping at a twig. They flinch.

– Put Him Down, like the animal he is.

Pause.

Whereas the SCUM – that apologise for them – and protect them – and hide them in places where good, decent people live – they've got no excuse. Cos they should know better.

And if I was to ever get my hands on a pair of dirty traitors like that – I wouldn't just –

She makes the snapping gesture again. Again they flinch.

– put them down – no: that would be too quick. I'd want to make them *suffer* – like little abused kids *suffer*. And speaking as someone who grew up having her twat spanked by nuns on a daily basis, I'd say I was just the person to do it, wouldn't you?

Blunt } I suppose so.
Gobbel } Yes.

She moves in closer, circling behind them. They're terrified.

Gronya   Good. So we're all in agreement. Isn't that nice?

Gobbel   It's lovely.

Gronya   It's lovely. Good. So you would tell me if such a pair of traitors happened to be in the area, wouldn't you?

Blunt } (*nods*) Yes, absolutely.
Gobbel } (*nods*) Definitely, we would!

Gronya   Of course you would. And you'd tell me if there was a plan to smuggle out the pervert, wouldn't you?

Blunt } We would, if there was, of course – !
Gobbel } We'd sing like canaries, wouldn't we?'

Gronya   Good. So it shouldn't be any trouble to tell me why exactly you should 'so coincidentally happen' to be 'here' 'of all places' on a quiet Christmas Eve, now should it?

Pause.

Blunt   We'd like to, honestly, but we simply just can't!

Gronya   Right. But *you* can know, can't you, and Tony *Blair* can know and the bloody social workers can know, but *us* – the people that have to *live* here – we're not *allowed* to know, are we? Cos we can't be *trusted* with that information, can we?

Blunt   Look – with respect – I understand your concerns but I promise you, you've got the wrong end of the stick. Hasn't she?

Gobbel   She has, she really has –

Blunt   I mean, if you knew how wrong you were –

Gobbel   She can't see the wood for the trees.

Blunt   It's actually almost funny, isn't it?

Gobbel   It *is* funny!

Blunt   Forgive me but it is –

Gobbel   It's hilarious!

Blunt   If only we could tell you how –

She knocks their helmets together, cutting off their laugher.

Gronya   Now you listen to me, you pair of nellies – my kid's got a spacesuit; it don't make him a fucking astronaut! So don't be thinking I'm squeamish. I've done for more pigs than Melton Mowbray and there's a bunk down Holloway the shape of my arse to prove it! So you tell me what you're doing here or I'll stuff your todgers so far up your bum'oles that every time you go pee-pee, you'll blow up like a pair of puffer fish!

Blunt   Now, just hold on a minute; you can't talk to us like that. We're Officers of the Law, and we've been trained to deal with tougher customers than you – haven't we?

Gobbel   When was that?

Blunt   What do you mean, 'when was that'?

Gobbel   Was that the week I was off with shingles?

Blunt   The point is that you don't scare us, Miss . . . Mrs. We can't tell you why we're here and even if we could, we wouldn't. So go ahead and do your worst, but I'll tell you this; our lips will remain absolutely *sealed*!

Gronya (*nods to* **Gobbel**)   And does that go for you too?

Gobbel   It goes *double* for –

Gronya *suddenly grabs their crotches in her vice-like fist, and* **Gobbel** *instantly screams:*

Gobbel   SHE'S DEAD!

Gronya   What?!

Gobbel   THE GIRL!

Blunt   Gobbel – shut up – !

Gronya   What girl?! Did the filthy nonce kill a girl?!

They shake their heads and manage a strangulated 'No'.

What then?! Tell me, or I swear to Christ, I'll go clockwise on you!

They are in terrible pain.

Gobbel   Blunt – I think – we should – tell her!

Blunt   We can't, it's – personal!

Gobbel   So – is *this*!

Gronya   What happened to the *girl*?!

She grips tighter. They scream.

Blunt   An accident – on the road – !

Gronya   On the road?!

Blunt   Coming home!

Gronya   On the road coming home?!

Blunt   That's why we're here –

Gobbel   To tell them –

Blunt   That their daughter died – !

Gobbel   On the way home – !

Blunt/Gobbel   For Christmas!

Pause. She lets them go and they fall to their knees.

Gronya   For Christmas?

They nod, kneading at their groins, dealing with the pain.

Gronya   That better not be a cover story. I know how you lot operate; you make up a cover story so you can smuggle them out!

Blunt   It's true, I swear.

Pause.

Gronya   You better not be lying. Not about a thing like that.

Pause.

You've heard nothing 'bout this paedo?

Blunt *shakes his head.*

Gronya   You don't know who he is? Or where he lives, or anything about him?

Blunt   Don't you?

In the background, the distant sound of the crowd chanting. **Gronya** *almost sniffs the air.*

Gronya   We will. Don't you worry. We've got friends in high places and they're on it right now. So tell your mates not to bother – this one's not slipping the net. Lynching him'll be our Christmas present to kids everywhere; the gift that keeps on giving.

Pause.

Have a nice Christmas.

Gobbel (*still recovering*)   And you!

Gronya *leaves.* **Blunt** *stares at* **Gobbel**. *Pause.*

Gobbel   What?

Blunt   'And you'!

Pause.

Gobbel   Just being polite . . .

Blunt   I can't feel my legs, can you?

Gobbel *crawls over and feels* **Blunt**'s *legs.*

Blunt   Not mine – yours!

Gobbel *feels his own legs.*

Blunt   Not with your hands!

Gobbel   What else am I going to feel them with?!

Blunt *rises, painfully, to his feet.*

Blunt   If you'd rung that bell when I told you, none of that would've happened.

Gobbel   It was you that stopped me!

Blunt   Well, I'm not stopping you now. Let's get it done and get out of harm's way.

Pause.

Gobbel   What do I say again?

Blunt   Don't you remember *anything*?

Pause.

Blunt   First, confirm identity.

Gobbel   Yes, that's right. 'Could you confirm that you know a person by the name of . . .'

Blunt *looks at the piece of paper.*

Blunt   Caroline Conner.

Gobbel   Caroline Conner –

Blunt (*nods*)   And they say 'Yes . . . ?'

Gobbel   Oh uh – (*Remembering.*) Please state your exact relationship to the deceased.

Blunt   Not 'the deceased'!

Gobbel (*pause*)   Who then?

Blunt   Say her name! Not 'the deceased'; they don't know she's deceased yet, do they?!

Gobbel   Please state your exact relationship to Miss Conner.

Blunt   And they say 'Parents' – And you say . . . ?

Gobbel   May we come in for a moment?

Blunt (*nods*)   'What's all this about, Officer?'

Gobbel   I'm afraid we have some . . . bad news. For you.

Pause.

Blunt   Prepare yourself . . .

Gobbel   I'm afraid you'll have to prepare yourself for . . . a shock.

Pause. They stare at each other, the horror of it dawning.

Gobbel   I'm sorry to inform you . . .

Blunt   . . . that your . . .

Gobbel   That your . . . daughter . . .

Blunt   That she's been . . .

Gobbel   That your daughter's been . . .

Pause. **Gobbel** *gasps like a fish.* **Blunt** *is also stricken with fear.*

Blunt! This is terrible!

Blunt   I know; but we have to do it. We can't go back not having done it. Our careers would be over before they've even begun!

Gobbel   Can't we just say they weren't in?

Blunt   Are you joking? The sarge'd peel our skulls like two satsumas. No – we have to tell them. Just remember; not the stormy seas around us . . .

Gobbel (*nods*)   The camel racing ahead.

Blunt   Exactly.

Blunt *gently ushers him towards the door.*

Gobbel   The camel racing ahead, the camel racing ahead, the camel racing ahead . . .

Pause. He nods grimly.

Right.

He straightens himself. Pause.

Are you ready?

Pause. **Blunt** *nods solemnly.*

Agonisingly slow, **Gobbel**'s *finger stretches out, just touching the skin of the bell. His arm trembles.*

Blunt   Press it –

Gobbel   I'm trying – !

Blunt   What do you mean, trying?!

Gobbel   I'm trying but I can't – !

Blunt   Why not? What's wrong?

Gobbel   My finger's too short!

Blunt   Why, you – !

Blunt *grabs* **Gobbel**'s *arm and presses it into the bell.*

The bell explodes in a puff of smoke and rings continuously; it's hideously shrill.

Blunt *and* **Gobbel** *run around like panicked sheep in a tiny pen, trying to get the thing to stop.*

Gobbel *takes his shoe off and starts hammering at it. Finally, it stops. The mechanism falls off the door frame.*

Pause. All composure gone, they quake in front of the door.

Blunt   Oh, my nerves – !

Gobbel   I've forgotten what I'm suppose to say!

Blunt   Put your shoe back on!

Gobbel   The camel racing ahead, the camel racing ahead, the camel racing ahead –

Blunt   Wait – shh! (*Pause.*) Can you hear anything?

Gobbel *shakes his head. Pause.*

Gobbel   Maybe there's no one in!

They put their heads to the door, listening. Pause.

There's no one in!

Joyous, he grabs **Blunt** *by the shoulders.*

Blunt, we're saved! There's no one in! We're – !

Above the door, a light comes on.

Pause. Their shoulders slump in resignation. They look at each other.

Blunt   We'll get through it.

Gobbel   Together?

Pause.

Blunt   Yes. Together.

Their arms creep around each other's backs.

A shape behind the glass.

The sound of locks opening. One, two, three . . .

And then the door swings open.

A small woman stands before them, older and more fragile than they could ever have imagined. Her hair is already shock-white. She stares at them with bulging eyes.

A frozen moment until **Blunt** *nudges* **Gobbel**.

Gobbel   Mrs Conner – ?

Pause.

Garson   She's dead, isn't she?!

They're stunned.

My little girl is dead, isn't she?!

Pause. She grabs **Gobbel** *by the lapels.*

TELL ME!

Gobbel   Yes! Yes! She's dead!

Pause. **Garson** *pushes* **Gobbel** *away and wanders out into the street.*

Garson   I knew it – I felt it in my heart – in here – I felt her leave this world – !

She sways slightly.

Blunt   We're very, very sorry, Mrs Conner.

A man's voice from inside.

Balthasar (*off*)   What is it, dear?! What's wrong?!

Bathasar, *her husband, appears. He is astoundingly old too.*

What's happened?

Garson   She's dead! Our little girl is dead!

Balthasar   Dead?!

He looks at **Blunt** *and* **Gobbel**.

Blunt   I'm afraid so.

Balthasar   Oh no –

He supports his sobbing wife.

Balthasar   How?

Blunt (*pause*)   An accident. On the road.

Garson *lets out a terrible moan and sags in his arms.*

Balthasar   Oh no, Garson – !

Gobbel   She's dead, Blunt! We've killed her!

Garson   My baby girl!

Blunt   Should we call an ambulance?

Balthasar   No, no, I just need to sit her down –

Blunt   Of course, yes.

Balthasar *escorts his weeping wife back down the hall.*

Blunt *goes to help but* **Gobbel** *stops him.*

Gobbel   Blunt –

Blunt   What?

Gobbel   She knew.

Blunt   We need to go and help him –

Gobbel   But how did she know?

Blunt (*pause*)   I suppose there's just things a mother knows. No explaining them, is there?

Pause. **Gobbel** *shrugs.*

Sorry.

Again, **Gobbel** *shrugs.*

Blunt   Come on then.

They go in, closing the door behind them.

Act Two

The living room.

It's very much an old person's home in ornament and design, though with well-travelled Bohemian overtones.

A large sash sags from the roof saying: 'Welcome Home Dearest Daughter'.

A Christmas tree with presents under it.

Balthasar *has sat* **Garson** *down on the sofa and is feeding her whisky in an attempt to calm her.*

Blunt *and* **Gobbel** *enter, awkwardly, at a loss*

Garson   I told you, didn't I? I said –

Balthasar   Ssshh now – drink this –

Garson   I saw it – something terrible, I said, something terrible, and you didn't believe me!

Balthasar   It's all right, dear, it'll be all right –

She pushes the whisky away.

Garson   No it won't! Nothing'll ever be all right again!

Balthasar   Shush now – I'm here –

Garson   I don't want *you*! What good are you?! I just want my baby back! My sweet little baby girl!

As she sobs, **Blunt** *and* **Gobbel** *can only look at the floor. She begins to shudder.*

Balthasar   We all want her back, dear. We all do.

Garson   Don't you lie to me! You never gave a damn about her or me or anyone!

She breaks away from **Balthasar** *and approaches* **Blunt** *and* **Gobbel**.

She was so beautiful, so – beautiful! If you'd seen her – her beautiful eyes – I saw them, those beautiful eyes but blind and lifeless – lifeless!

She grabs their hands.

And I felt her – felt her leave this world – like they lift a baby from your arms – felt her die, in here!

She presses their hands to her belly.

Balthasar   I'm sure they understand, dear – come on now –

He gently takes her shoulders, but she resists.

Garson   Don't believe him – he never loved her – never loved me – he'll smile and smile but don't believe him, he's a liar, he's –

And she faints in his arms. **Blunt** *helps* **Balthasar** *support her.*

Gobbel   That's it, she's dead!

I told you, Blunt – we've killed her stone dead!

Blunt   Stop saying that! She's not *dead*!

She's not, is she?!

Garson *groans.*

Balthasar   No, no, I think it's just the shock. I think she just needs a lie-down.

Blunt   Why don't we call an ambulance?

Garson   No!

Balthasar   No, officer, really. She doesn't like doctors at the best of times. I just need to get her to the bedroom, lie her down for a while.

Blunt *helps them stand.*

Balthasar   That's it, I've got her.

Blunt   I'll help you.

Balthasar   No, it's fine – she can manage – you can manage can't you, dear?

Blunt   It's no trouble.

Blunt *opens the door for them.*

Balthasar   No, thank you, but she doesn't like strangers in the bedroom. I can manage, really. You have a seat, I'll be back in a moment. Come on, dear . . .

Blunt   Don't you worry about us.

Balthasar *escorts his wife away. The door closes, leaving* **Blunt** *and* **Gobbel**.

Blunt   A lot of help *you* were!

Gobbel   I think we should call for an ambulance.

Blunt   You heard what he said; she doesn't like doctors.

Gobbel   She didn't look too good.

Blunt   Well, you wouldn't, would you? (*Pause.*) Wait till he gets back; see what he says.

Pause. They exchange a grim look.

Awful.

Gobbel   Terrible.

They sit down, **Blunt** *in the armchair,* **Gobbel** *on the sofa. Pause.*

They look old for fifty.

Blunt *scowls at him. Pause.*

Gobbel *stares up at the sash.*

Gobbel   Look at that.

Blunt (*nods*)   Awful.

Gobbel   D'you reckon?

Pause. **Blunt** *sees* **Gobbel** *still staring upwards.*

Blunt   Not the *sash*. The *situation*.

Gobbel   Oh – yes; awful.

Pause.

Gobbel   I can't imagine anything worse.

Blunt   No.

Pause.

Apart from murder. When a child's murdered, that's worse.

Gobbel (*nods*)   Apart from that, you're right. Nothing worse than a child being murdered.

Pause.

Blunt   Suicide, maybe.

Gobbel   D'you reckon?

Blunt (*nods*)   On a par.

Gobbel (*nods*)   On the mother too.

Pause.

Blunt   I mean the *same*. On a *par*.

Gobbel (*nods*)   Both of them.

Blunt *sighs, shaking his head*.

Gobbel   Gav said he was on a suicide the other week, did he tell you?

Blunt (*nods*)   Awful.

Gobbel   What was the story with that?

Blunt   Oh, some kid playing on a Ouija board. Thought the devil had possessed him. Ended up hanging himself. Only thirteen he was. Awful.

Gobbel (*shakes head*)   Terrible.

Pause.

Wonder what Rolf Harris thinks of that.

Blunt   Rolf Harris?

Gobbel   Well, he must've got it off him, mustn't he?
Never seen anyone else play one.

Pause.

Blunt   'Wobbleboard'.

Gobbel   Eh?

Blunt   Rolf Harris plays a 'wobbleboard'.

Pause.

Gobbel   What did *you* say?

Blunt (*sighs*)   Never mind.

Pause.

Gobbel   He seems a nice old fellow, doesn't he?

Blunt *shrugs in agreement.*

Gobbel   Doesn't seem fair, does it?

Blunt   It's always the way. The cruel and reckless shoot to
the top. It's the kind ones get it in the neck. I'm living proof
of that.

Gobbel   You mean like Racquel leaving you for the hot-
dog man?

Blunt   Do you have to keep bringing that up?

Gobbel *shrugs an apology. Pause.*

Blunt   Of course, you know what he was before he was a
hot-dog seller?

Gobbel (*pause*)   Single?

Blunt *stares at him. Pause.*

Blunt Apart from that. (*Pause.*) A bullfighter. Which proves what I said about the cruel. Mind you, I suppose it'd come in handy, given her temper.

Gobbel If you ask me, you're better off without her.

Blunt Not really; a year later she made half a million pounds on the stock market.
(*Pause.*) Still – I'd rather be kind and get nowhere than successful and cruel.

Gobbel Me too.

Blunt *snorts.*

Gobbel What?

Again, **Blunt** *snorts.*

Gobbel I'm not going to get anywhere!
Where do you think I'm going to get to?

Blunt Nowhere . . .

Gobbel (*pause*) You're just saying that.

Blunt Not at all. In fact, in your case, even getting nowhere might be setting the sights too high.

Gobbel D'you reckon?

Blunt Absolutely.

Pause. **Gobbel** *hugs* **Blunt**.

What are you doing?!

Gobbel That's the nicest thing anyone ever said to me!

Blunt *pats him uncomfortably, trying to shift him.*

Blunt Yes, well, that's – good –

Gobbel Happy Christmas, Blunt – !

Blunt Yes, and you – now –

Gobbel   I wouldn't rather go nowhere with anyone else but you!

Balthasar *comes in, catching them in the hug.*

Balthasar   Oh – excuse me –

Blunt *casts* **Gobbel** *off and stands.*

Blunt   Oh, Mr Conner, no, he's just – a bit 'upset' about – your situation. We both are.

Balthasar   Well, that's very . . . very *kind* of you . . . yes.

Gobbel   How's his wife?

Blunt   How's Mrs Conner?

Balthasar   Oh, well, she's having a little sleep just now –

Gobbel   Are you sure?

Balthasar   Am I – ?

Gobbel   Are you sure she's asleep?

Balthasar   Am I sure – ? Oh, yes, no; I'm sure she's asleep, yes . . .

Blunt   Excuse our concern; it's just that shock can sometimes be dangerous. Especially when the person in shock is, well . . .

Gobbel   Old!

Blunt   Where are your manners?

Balthasar   Oh no, really, officer, no need. You don't get to this age without being old.

Blunt   No, quite. But you're sure we shouldn't call a doctor? Maybe some sedatives would help.

Balthasar   No, that's very kind, but really; she's not much truck with that sort of thing. If it can't be scraped off bark, she won't take it, bless her. But she's a tough old bird, that's for sure. Got that way in the Blitz. Ten years old and shifting rubble she was; still the same skin on her hands.

Tough old bird for sure.
Anyway, I must thank you, Constable . . . ?

Blunt   Blunt.

They shake hands.

Balthasar   How do you do?

Blunt   And this is my colleague, Constable Gobbel.

Balthasar   How do you do?

They shake hands.

Gobbel   No, how do *you*?

Balthasar   Balthasar.

Gobbel   No, *Gobbel.*

Balthasar   Gobb – ? (*Pause.*) Oh – no, that's me; *I'm*
Balthasar –

Gobbel   Oh – !

Balthasar   Sorry, I didn't make myself clear –

Blunt   It's not you; his helmet's a little tight.

Balthasar   His – ? Oh well, anyway, as I was saying – I
must thank you for all your kindness. It can't be pleasant
having to deliver such news, and tonight of all nights.

Blunt   No, well, you're right; it's a grim task but –
ultimately it's a matter of duty. We just want you to know
how very sorry we are for your sad and tragic loss.

Balthasar   Well, thank you, Officer, I appreciate that; for
my wife, more so than for me.

Pause. **Blunt** *and* **Gobbel** *look a bit puzzled.*

That must sound terrible, mustn't it? It's not that I'm not
sad, I am, it's just that, well – she wasn't actually *mine*, you
see . . .

Blunt/Gobbel   'Ohhh' . . . !

Balthasar   It probably shouldn't make a difference, should it? It's just that I never had much contact with her, to be honest. Or rather, she never had much contact with me, I don't know why. Never really accepted me. Bit jealous, I think, though goodness knows why. It's not as if I got between them. No one ever did.

Pause.

Forgive me; I'm sure you've got better things to do than listen to some old fool get maudlin . . .

Blunt   Not at all –

Gobbel   It's a pleasure.

Balthasar   You're very kind. (*Pause.*) It's time, you see? You'd think at this age you'd treat every minute like gold. But you don't; you still think you've time for everything.

Pause as they respectfully absorb this.

Blunt   Speaking of which, there are a few minor details I'm afraid we have to –

Gobbel   Blunt!

The living-room door swings open to reveal **Garson** *standing there, wide-eyed and mad-looking, staring right at* **Blunt** *and* **Gobbel**.

Blunt   Mrs Conner!

Balthasar *turns and sees her. She doesn't like the look of him.*

Balthasar   Oh now – what are you doing up?

Pause.

Blunt   How are you feeling?

Pause. Her face softens into a charming smile.

Garson   Why, thank you for asking, Captain, but I'm fine now. I always get a little sick approaching Gibraltar, I don't know why.

She pushes an imaginary trolley towards them.

Balthasar   Oh no, dear – come on now –

Garson   Would you and the Viceroy care for some tea?

Balthasar   No, dear; the Captain's had some tea –
I'm terribly sorry; she goes a little funny sometimes,
especially under stress. Come back to your cabin for now,
dear –

He puts his arms at her shoulders and she turns on him.

Garson   Get your hands off of me, you *prick*!

He recoils. Again, she smiles and turns to **Blunt** *and* **Gobbel**.

Will Darjeeling do?

She holds up an imaginary teapot.

Garson   Cups, gentlemen?

They look to **Balthasar**.

Balthasar   I'm terribly sorry but it's probably best to
just . . .

Pause. They do so – **Blunt**, *awkwardly, but* **Gobbel**, *fairly
naturally.*

*Pause. They raise imaginary cups, and she pretend pours them a cup of
tea.*

Garson   Cream and sugar?

Blunt   Um – no, that's fine for me, thank you.

Gobbel   Just sugar for me.

*She scoops out an imaginary spoonful of sugar and is about to put it in
the imaginary cup when* **Blunt** *blocks her.*

Blunt   That'll be fine as it is, thank you. We don't want
the Viceroy losing all his 'teeth', now do we?

Garson (*to* **Gobbel**)   Ooh, he's a harsh one, that Captain,
isn't he? But he's not all rules and regulations below deck,
are you, sir?

Gobbel   Isn't he?

Blunt   Amn't I?

Garson   Put it this way; every time we girls go into his cabin he just happens to be in the altogether, don't you, sir?

Balthasar   Oh no, dear, please . . .

Gobbel *looks suspiciously at* **Blunt**.

Garson   I'm sure it's coincidence but there's some of the girls not so sure. One of them's taken to walking in backwards, so I heard. Naughty Captain!

She prods his stomach. **Gobbel** *still staring at him.*

Under the eyes of suspicion, **Blunt** *pretends to drink his tea. He meets* **Gobbel***'s gaze.*

Blunt (*pause*)   *What?*

Balthasar   All right now, dear; they've got their tea – let's be getting you back to your cabin –

She pulls away from his gently guiding hand.

Garson   Who are you?!

Balthasar   You know who I am, dear; now let's not make a scene –

Garson   You're not a passenger on this ship! You're not crew! Captain – this man is a stowaway!

Blunt   No –

Garson   He is! He shouldn't be here –

Blunt   He's not a stowaway, he's your husband –

Garson   What do you mean, my husband? I'm not married?! (*Pause.*) What's going on here?

Blunt   He's only here to look after you. I give you my word as Captain.

Garson   Do you?

Gobbel   And mine as Viceroy.

Balthasar *puts his hand on her shoulder. Unsure, she begins to acquiesce.*

Balthasar   Come on, dear, please . . .

Garson   Will the gentlemen require anything further?

Blunt   No – thank you. That'll be all.

Garson   Then if you don't mind, sir, I will retire to my cabin for a spell. I've lost my beautiful baby, you see, and I'm a little out of sorts.

Gobbel   Carry on.

Garson   Thank you, sir. I'm sure I'll be my old self again by evening.

Balthasar   That's right, dear; come along . . .

He starts to lead her out.

Gobbel   Don't forget your trolley!

Garson   Oh!

She returns to collect her trolley.

Silly me.

She wheels it out.

Balthasar   I'm terribly sorry about all this – You're not in a rush, are you?

Blunt (*pause*)   Um – no, not at all. You go ahead.

Balthasar *exits.*

Blunt *stares very deliberately at* **Gobbel**.

Blunt   'Don't forget your trolley'?!

Pause. **Gobbel** *shrugs, ashamed.* **Blunt** *shakes his head, at a loss. He sits down.*

Gobbel   Poor old Mrs Conner.

Blunt   It's not good that. Once they start going like that
. . . beginning of the end.

Gobbel   D'you reckon?

Blunt   This'll only speed it up. Awful.

Gobbel   Terrible. Poor old Balthasar.

Pause.

It's sad he didn't get on with his daughter.

Blunt   But she wasn't his daughter, was she? That's why
they didn't get on.

Gobbel   My parents weren't my parents either, I still got
on with them.

Blunt   I thought you didn't?

Gobbel   I don't get on with them *now*. But I used to.

Blunt   So when did you stop getting on with them?

Gobbel   When they told me they weren't my parents.

Blunt *looks puzzled. Puzzlement turns to anger.*

Blunt   Right – that's it! When he comes back, you're
going to fix a time for him to come and identify the body
and then we're leaving, before I lose what's left of my mind!

Gobbel (*pause*)   Wait a minute – I have to –

Blunt   Of course –

Gobbel   No, no – I had to ring the bell and I had to tell
them but that's not part of telling them –

Blunt   I don't remember you telling anyone anything!

Gobbel   I did so!

Blunt   She guessed it!

Gobbel   But then I confirmed it.

Blunt   Only because she shook it out of you. And then you stood there gasping like a fish while I did everything else!

Gobbel   That's a rotten lie! I rang the bell and I told them and now it's as much your turn as mine! And that's the living end of it!

Pause. **Blunt** *nods, disappointed.*

Blunt   I see.

This always works – **Gobbel** *visibly crumbles.*

Gobbel   What?

Blunt   Look at that tree.

He points commandingly. **Gobbel** *doesn't look.*

Gobbel   Why?

Blunt   Look at it!

Pause. **Gobbel** *looks at the tree.*

Look at those presents.
Look how lovingly they've been wrapped.
You think those presents will ever be opened?

Pause.

Gobbel   We can't open them . . . ?

Blunt   Of course we can't! That's my point; *No One Ever Will.* Those presents will stay wrapped. Weeks will turn to months, months will turn to years. And still they'll sit there, waiting, as the colours fade, waiting, as the dust gathers, for ever waiting . . . for the Child That Will Never Come.

Pause.

Gobbel   Poor presents . . .

Blunt   Never mind the presents – what about that old lady through there, demented with grief?! Old Balthasar that you say you feel so sorry for! But here you are arguing about

whose *turn* it is! And you've the cheek to call yourself kind!
Why the word's like dust in your mouth!

Gobbel   I am kind! You're the one that's not kind and I'm
just as kind as you, if not kinder!

Blunt   Well, we'll see about that, shall we?

Gobbel   Yes, we shall!

Blunt   Right – well, I'm going to the toilet. And when I
come back I'll expect you to have concluded our business
here!

Gobbel   Fine!

Blunt   Fine!

Gobbel *goes to the door. He peers cautiously out. Pause.*

Gobbel   Blunt?

Blunt *stops, looks at him.*

Gobbel   Is a viceroy better than a captain?

Blunt   *NO!*

Blunt *exits.*

Gobbel *is left to mutter and sulk.*

Gobbel   Think you're so kind, but you're not . . . not kind
to me . . . I'll show you . . . We'll see who's kind . . . Yes, sir
– we need you to come and identify your daughter's body
. . . yes, as soon as possible . . . Tomorrow? Yes, that would
be ideal . . . *Thank you, you've been very kind* . . . Not at all,
sir . . . *No, but much kinder than the other one . . . glad it was you
that told me, not him . . . probably my wife would be dead now if it
hadn't been you, probably would have dropped dead right there on the
spot* – Oh really, sir, please . . . *No, no I insist, I'll be telling the
sarge all about it – I wouldn't be surprised if you get promoted there
and then – and have a present too – have the biggest present there with
love from me and my wife because actually we're your parents –*
You're my? – *Yes, we're your actual parents and all this has just*

been a big thing to get you here so we can tell you – No! *– Yes, and all these presents are actually for you but we just had to find out if you were the kindest one –*

Balthasar *returns.*

Balthasar   I'm terribly sorry (to have kept you) –

Gobbel *jumps, spilling presents.*

Gobbel   Dad! Oh – sorry – I was just –

Pause.

Balthasar   Has the other constable gone?

Gobbel   Oh – um – just – to the toilet.

Balthasar   Oh. I hope he's found it. Bit of a funny layout, this house. Mind you, I suppose if a policeman can't find the toilet I don't know who can!

He laughs. **Gobbel** *jollies along.*

Balthasar *pours himself a drink.*

Balthasar   You must excuse my wife. She gets a little confused now and then –

Gobbel *sees* **Blunt** *appear outside the window, looking a bit confused. He holds up his hands in bemusement, then wanders away.*

Balthasar   I keep telling her she should go and see a doctor about it but of course she won't hear of it. It doesn't happen that often but it does make her not act herself and it can all be a little embarrassing at times . . .

Gobbel *nods sympathetically, looking for a chance to say what he has to say.*

Balthasar   She worked on a cruise liner, you see, and this is, oh – some forty years gone – but sometimes she gets the idea she's back on it. I don't know why. It was only a few months of her life, so I don't know why it's so significant to her. I mean, we hadn't even met by then. Still, time like this, maybe it's good not to know what's going on.

Pause.

Gobbel   I'm awfully sorry about what's happened.

Balthasar   Yes, thank you . . .

Gobbel   And I'm sorry we had to tell you.

Balthasar   Oh no, really, you mustn't. It's not your fault.

Gobbel   It isn't, is it?

Balthasar   Of course not, not at all. These things happen. She'll get over it in time.

Gobbel   D'you reckon?

Balthasar   Oh yes, like I said, she's a tough old bird. She's had her share of tragedy across the years. Lost her brother, Theo, in the war . . . Her younger sister, Fenella, she died of malaria. Martha, she went over a cliff in that caravan . . .

Pause.

Her nephew, Harold – he was electrocuted. Her best friend died of a jellyfish sting. And then her parents – both of them to cancer, so yes . . . She's had her share.

Pause.

Gordon, her other brother, he died of pneumonia and his wife caught it off him and she died too and her Uncle Callum, they never even found him. But she survived all that and if you can survive all that then she'll survive this. I mean, as harsh as it sounds and as much as she loved her, at the end of the day, it's only a dog, isn't it?

Pause. **Gobbel**'*s face freezes over.*

Blunt *enters.*

Balthasar   Ah there you are – did you find it all right?

Blunt   Yes, thank you – Has my colleague discussed the matters I mentioned with you?

Gobbel *is staring at* **Blunt**, *frozen in horror.*

Balthasar   Matters?

Blunt   I can see from his expression that he has not. So it would seem that it is, once again, down to me!

Gobbel   No, wait – !

Blunt   I don't want to hear your excuses, Constable. I've had my fill of them this evening –

Gobbel   No, but Blunt – !

Blunt   We – will discuss it – LATER.

Pause. **Gobbel** *sits down, face in hands.*

Now, as I was saying; I'm afraid that before we can conclude our business, there are a few routine, though unhappy, procedural matter we must attend to. The most pressing of which, I'm afraid, is the matter of identification.

Balthasar   Oh . . . .

Blunt   I'm afraid so.

Balthasar   Will a pension book do?

Pause.

Blunt   Oh, no, no – not you – We know who you are. No, I mean identification of – the *deceased*.

Balthasar   The – ? Oh, right – well – is there any need for that?

Pause.

I mean, you say it's her and I'm quite happy to take your word for it . . .

Pause.

Blunt   Well, I appreciate your confidence, but that's not exactly –

Gobbel *tugs at his sleeve.*

Gobbel   Blunt – !

Blunt   *I* – AM NOT *SPEAKING* – TO *YOU!*

Gobbel *retreats.*

Blunt   I'm afraid it's standard procedure; someone always has to identify the body.

Balthasar   Oh, I see – It's just I'd rather not put her through that, you understand – not in her present condition –

Blunt   Oh, but it needn't be your wife . . .

Balthasar   No?

Blunt   No, no; just someone who knew the deceased. You'd do as well –

Balthasar   Me . . . ? (*Pause.*) I don't want to be difficult, Officer, really I don't, but is this absolutely necessary?

Blunt   I'm afraid so. As strange as it may seem, mistakes have been made. It's highly unusual, but it has been known, so . . .

Balthasar   Yes, I see. It just seems – (*Pause.*) I mean, she's going grey, isn't she?

Pause.

Blunt   Well, that does tend to happen –

Balthasar   Bad teeth – one broken at the front?

Pause.

Long, very prominent teats.

Pause. **Blunt** *clears throat.*

Blunt   I'm afraid I wouldn't have any of that information, sir . . .

Balthasar   Oh dear – I'm sure it's her. Long-haired but patchy – you know; down below –

Blunt   Down below?!

Balthasar   Yes, you know . . . smells a bit mangy –

Blunt   Mr Conner, please! (*Pause.*) Now I know you weren't close but there's such a thing as respect for the dead. I doubt Mrs Conner would appreciate you talking in such a fashion, now, would she?

Balthasar   Well, no – she wouldn't. But then I was the only one who smelt it –

Blunt   I beg your pardon?!

Balthasar   Well, me and the postman. I think he smelt it, though he never actually said –

Blunt   Do you realise what you're saying?

Balthasar   I don't see what the fuss is –

Blunt (*to* **Gobbel**)   He doesn't see what the fuss is!

Gobbel   But Blunt –

Blunt   Be quiet! You don't see what the fuss is?

Balthasar   Well, not really, no, I mean – she's dead, isn't she?

Blunt   And so?

Balthasar   Well, we're not going to have her stuffed or anything –

Blunt   There's no need for sarcasm.

Balthasar   Well, can't you just burn her and be done with it?

Blunt   Burn her and be – ?!

Pause.

Well, well, well! And to think my colleague and I were only just saying how cruel fate was to the kind. But once again our compassionate natures have been deceived!

Come, Constable. We've done our duty here. Please give our condolences to your good lady wife.

Balthasar   But she's a dog!?

Blunt   Nonetheless – please convey them.

As they approach the door, **Gobbel** *gets his attention.*

For God's sake, what is it?!

Gobbel *whispers in his ear.*

The penny drops. **Blunt** *seizes* **Gobbel***'s shoulder. They stand frozen for some time.*

Balthasar   Look, I'm terribly sorry, Officer, I seem to have offended you somehow – I like dogs, really I do, I just –

Pause. **Blunt** *turns to him.*

Blunt   Dogs.

Balthasar (*pause*)   Well, what do *you* call them?

Pause. He is at a loss.

I tell you what; our daughter Carol's due any minute and it was her that gave us the dog, so she knows what it looks like. She might be a bit tired because she's driving here from Bristol, but I'm sure she could do whatever has to be done. How about that?

Pause.

Blunt   Dog.

Pause.

Yes, you see – Mr Conner – Balthasar – It would seem that there's been a small . . .

Pause.

Actually, quite a *large* . . . misunderstanding.

Balthasar (*pause*)   Misunderstanding?

Blunt Yes, you see – you're talking about . . . a dog.

Balthasar *nods.*

Blunt Which went . . . missing, did it?

Balthasar Yes, about a week ago.

Pause.

Why? What's wrong?

Pause.

Blunt Well, you see . . . the thing is . . . what we're talking about . . .

Balthasar *looks a little pained, as you might with indigestion.*

Balthasar Yes . . . ?

Blunt Well, you see – you're talking about . . . a dog . . .

Balthasar *nods through another twinge. He rubs his chest.*

Blunt Whereas what we're actually talking about . . .

Balthasar *groans a little.*

Gobbel What's wrong with him?

Blunt What's wrong with you?

Balthasar *(pained)* I'm fine; go on –

Blunt He's fine.

Gobbel So why's he rubbing his chest like that?

Blunt Why are you rubbing your chest like that?

Balthasar It's nothing, just a twinge; what you're talking about is what?

Blunt What we're talking about is . . .

Another twinge, worse, and **Balthasar** *has to sit down.*

Balthasar Oh dear –

They help him.

Blunt   Are you all right?

Balthasar   Yes, yes, really; I just . . . just need a little . . . sit-down . . .

Gobbel   He's gone all white!

Balthasar   I wonder if you'd be so kind as to pass me . . . that pill bottle . . . on the sideboard . . .

Gobbel   Pill bottle!?

Blunt   Pill bottle on the sideboard!

Gobbel *gets the bottle.*

Gobbel   They're tiny, Blunt! Tiny pills!

He gives it to **Blunt***, who gives it to* **Balthasar***.*

That's bad, Blunt – tiny pills are bad! Why does he need tiny pills?!

Balthasar *shakes his head, trying to unscrew the top.*

Balthasar   Do you think you could . . . ?

He passes the bottle to **Blunt** *to open.*

Gobbel   What's wrong with him?!

Balthasar   I'm fine, I just –

Blunt   He's fine!

Blunt *passes* **Balthasar** *a pill.*

Gobbel   He doesn't look fine – !

Blunt   Do you need some water?

Balthasar *shakes his head, puts the pill in his mouth, swallows it.*
Pause.

Gobbel   He's skin's all grey and baggy!

Blunt   Of course it is! (*Pause.*) I mean – Will you be
'quiet'?! Let the man recover!

Balthasar *exhales.*

Blunt   That's it. Just relax. Deep breath in. Deep breath
out. Deep breath in. Deep breath out.

Gobbel *breathes along but exhales on the in and inhales on the out.*

Blunt   Deep breath in. Deep breath out. Deep breath in.
Deep breath out.

Balth *starts to breathe heavier, put off by* **Gobbel**.

Blunt   Deep breath in. Deep breath – will you stop that?!

Gobbel   Stop what?

Blunt   Stop breathing!

Gobbel   Stop breathing?!

Blunt   Stop breathing out of time! It's messing 'me' up,
never mind him!

Gobbel   I got off to a bad start.

Balthasar   I'll be fine now, really. I'll be fine . . .

Blunt   Are you sure?

Balthasar   Oh yes, really. Just a little twinge, that's all. I
get them if I don't take my pill on time. But I'll be fine now,
thank you . . . (*Pause.*) Thank you.

Gobbel   What's wrong with you?

Blunt   I don't think that's our business, do you?

Balthasar   No, no, I don't mind. Just a little trouble with
the old ticker, Constable; another pleasure of old age.

Blunt   But nothing too serious?

Balthasar   Well . . . Three heart attacks in the last two
years.

Blunt   Three?!

Gobbel   That's nearly one a year!

Balthasar (*nods*)   They offered me a pacemaker but I didn't fancy it. Be like you'd swallowed a clock, don't you think? Of course, the doctor thinks I'm mad. Says I should treat every day like my last.

Gobbel   Your last what?

Balthasar   Well-day, I suppose. But how you do that? I said, if it's all the same to you, I'd as soon treat my last day like all the rest. Seems more achievable, don't you think?

Pause.

Goodness – you look more worried than me! But he exaggerates, that doctor; I mean, according to him, my heart's so weak you could kill me just by creeping up behind me and bursting a paper bag!

Gobbel ⎫ A paper bag!
Blunt ⎭ A paper bag?!

Balthasar   A paper bag, can you imagine? I said, whatever you do, don't tell Garson, she'll be getting ideas. Be the perfect crime, wouldn't it?

Anyway – what was it you were saying?

Blunt   Saying . . .

Balthasar   You said I was talking about a dog but you were talking about . . . ?

Pause.

Gobbel   A victim!

Balthasar (*pause*)   A victim?

Pause.

Blunt   Yes, you see – you were talking about a dog . . . whereas to us, it's . . . a victim.

Gobbel   Of crime.

Balthasar   Oh . . .

Blunt   Yes; be it a dog or, or be it – um . . .

Gobbel (*pause*)   A non-dog –

Blunt   A non-dog, yes –

Balthasar   A non-dog?

Blunt   Yes – dog or non-dog, to us it makes no difference; they're all victims to us and we treat every case exactly the same.

Balthasar (*nods*)   Oh, I see. You'll have to excuse me, Officer. I'm a little behind on all this animal rights business. Growing up during the war, we were mainly worried about people. Still, I suppose it's the fashion these days.
So will that do? If Carol identifies the body?

Pause.

Blunt   Well – in 'principle', yes, it's just . . . You see, the thing is . . .

Balthasar   I'm expecting her any moment. She should have been here by now but I suppose the roads are busy; everyone coming home for Christmas. But I'd say it won't be more than fifteen minutes or so, so you're quite welcome to wait. What do you think?

Blunt (*pause*)   What do I think . . . ?

Blunt *looks at* **Gobbel***, who shrugs.*

Gobbel   If it's just fifteen minutes . . .

Balthasar   Then that's what we'll do. Would you like a drink at all? There's orange juice or tea if you fancy – I'd offer you something stronger but I suppose you're not allowed, are you?

Gobbel *looks hopefully at* **Blunt***.*

Balthasar   I won't tell if you won't.

Blunt   I suppose if it's just one . . .

Balthasar   That's the ticket – !

Gobbel   D'you reckon?

Blunt   How much worse can things get?

The doorbell rings. **Blunt** *and* **Gobbel** *stare at each other.*

Balthasar   Talk of the devil, there's Carol now! With all sorts of nonsense that'll need carrying in, if I know her. Just you help yourself to whatever you want. Now – Goodness, I'm a little nervous actually. She's been in Africa for three years with that what-d'you-call-them – ? the clothes shop – Oxfam, you know, so we haven't seen her . . . D'you think I should get Garson up? No – it'll be a surprise – How do I look?

They stare at him. Pause.

Old, I suppose.

Pause.

Blunt   Not at all.

The bell rings again.

Balthasar   Righty-ho . . . COMING, DEAR!

Balthasar *exits.*

Gobbel   Who do you think it is?

Blunt   I know who it's not.

Gobbel   But maybe it is, though! Maybe there's been a mistake! Maybe we've got the wrong house or something!

Blunt (*pause*)   No, I checked the number.

Gobbel (*pause*)   But maybe they got it wrong at the station – ! They might've, mightn't they?

Blunt   They might've . . .

Gobbel   So maybe it's her! Blunt – maybe she's alive!

Garson   Maybe who's alive?

Startled, they turn to see **Garson** *in the doorway again.*

Blunt   Mrs Conner – !

Garson   What's going on here?

Gobbel (*pause*)   There's someone at the door –

Garson   At the door?

Gobbel (*pause*)   At the front –

Blunt *stops him with a gesture that says 'Leave it to me'.*

Blunt   'Someone' – is 'boarding' – the 'ship'.

Pause.

Garson   What are you talking about, you stupid man? Where's that damn fool husband of mine?

Gobbel   He's gone ashore.

Garson   He's gone ashore?!

Blunt   He's gone 'to the door'.

Garson   Why?

Gobbel   Because there's someone at it.

Garson   I can see that. What are you doing here?

Pause.

Blunt   We came to tell you – you know – the bad news we told you . . .

She looks puzzled.

Don't you remember?

Pause.

Garson   My baby?

Blunt   Well . . . sort of.

Garson   My beautiful baby . . . (*Pause.*) She was so beautiful. So happy to see me. So scared when I was gone.

Pause. She looks at them.

Would you like to see my bum, mister?

Gobbel *leaps with surprise.*

Garson   I'll show you if you want, I don't mind.

She turns and starts to lift her skirt. **Blunt** *stops her, in a panic.*

Blunt   No, really, thank you but we're fine – !

Garson   I don't mind, really I don't –

Blunt   I'm sure, but really – don't you think you'd be best off having a little rest?!

He starts ushering her out the door.

Garson   Why?

Blunt   Well – your husband says it's –

Garson   My 'husband'! Who cares what he says, the gutless freak!

Blunt   I'm sure you don't mean that –

Garson   Oh no, of course not. After all, why would someone say something they meant? And how could they mean it about nice old Balthasar, right?

Gobbel   He's always been nice to us.

Garson   'Nice'! God protect us from 'nice'! And I suppose you're 'nice' too, are you?

Blunt   We try our best . . .

Garson   Yes, I can smell it on you. Like cheap soap.

Blunt   Well – you know what they say; it's nice to be nice.

Gobbel   To see you –

Blunt/Gobbel   Nice!

She turns her back to them and lifts her skirt.

Garson   Wheee!

They scream.

Blunt   Mrs Conner, please!

She hobbles away from them, trying to pull her tights down.

(*To* **Gobbel**.)   Help me get a hold of her!

They manage to grab her and try to pull her tights back up.

And just then, the vicar – **Reverend Shandy** *– enters.*

Shandy   What on earth?!

Blunt *and* **Gobbel** *stare at him in horror. Pause.*

Blunt   This isn't how it looks – !

Garson   How *does* it look?!

Balthasar *pushes past the vicar.*

Balthasar   Oh dear, I'm so sorry about this – ! Garson, dear, *please* try to control yourself!

Garson   Oh yes, cos we don't want a fuss, do we? No – nothing worse than a messy awful *fuss*!

Balthasar   No, but look, dear; the vicar's here –

This gets her attention.

Garson   Ah, the new vicar –

Shandy   Well, it's been a month or two, but yes –

He extends his hand.

Reverend Shandy. But you can call me Hans.

She doesn't take it.

Garson   I hear the last one left with his halo round his ankles. After all that nasty business at the raffle. But that's the liar's punishment, isn't it?

Balthasar   You're being a little rude, dear –

Garson   D'you know what that is, Reverend? The liar's punishment?

Shandy   According to Aesop, that he won't be believed, even when he speaks the truth.

Garson   No. That he can never believe anyone else, even when they speak the truth.

Shandy   That's very good. I'll remember that for a sermon.

Garson   Yes; a little sweetcorn in the turd.

Balthasar   Oh no, dear, please –

Shandy   It's all right, Mr Conner, I understand. As Euripides said, How dark are all the ways of God to man. Especially at a time such as this.

Blunt *and* **Gobbel** *exchange looks of dismay.*

Shandy   You will feel anger towards Him, Mrs Conner. You will wonder what purpose this tragedy serves in His Grand design –

Blunt   Yes, well, I was wondering that myself, weren't you?

Gobbel   Absolutely.

Blunt   What would the purpose of this tragedy be, do you think, Reverend?

Shandy   Well, that is for Him to know –

Gobbel   And us to find out.

Shandy   Yes, well – No: not for us to find out –

Blunt   So you don't know the purpose?

Shandy   No, but I know there is one –

Gobbel   How d'you know there's a purpose if you don't know what the purpose is?

Shandy   Because there's always a purpose, Constable – ?

Gobbel (*points to* **Blunt**)   Blunt.

Shandy (*to* **Gobbel**)   Blunt?

Blunt   No, I'm Blunt. He's Gobbel.

Gobbel   No, that's me.

Blunt   Have you met Balthasar?

Shandy   No, how do you – no, yes, of course I've met him!

Blunt   Good, well, thanks for stopping by –

Garson   My Baby! My Beautiful Baby!

Pause.

Gobbel (*to* **Shandy**)   So are you doing anything for Christmas?

Shandy   Step aside, Officer. That woman needs comfort.

He pushes past them. **Blunt** *and* **Gobbel** *watch in horror.* **Shandy** *takes her hand. This time she allows it.*

There, my dear. There.

Garson   I felt her. Felt her leave this world.

Shandy   All flesh is grass, and all the goodliness thereof is as the flower of the field.

Garson *rests her head against him.*

Balthasar   See now, isn't that nice, dear? The Father's come all the way here just to offer his condolences about Miffy.

Blunt *and* **Gobbel** *look at each other: saved!*

Balthasar   I keep telling her the Church isn't just for people who believe in God, but she – never listens, do you?

Shandy   Did you say Miffy?

Again, **Blunt** *and* **Gobbel** *look at each other: not saved.*

Balthasar   That's what we called her.

Shandy   Oh, a nickname . . . ?

Balthasar   No, just her name.

Shandy (*puzzled*)   Oh . . .

Balthasar   Why?

Shandy   No – just that wasn't the name the duty sergeant gave me.

Blunt   Duty sergeant?

Shandy   Yes, I was just calling the station to wish them a merry Christmas and she told me the unhappy news but I'm sure she gave another name –

Blunt   Oh, yes, well! The duty sergeant, she's just – always getting names wrong, isn't she?

Gobbel (*nods*)   Always!

Blunt   I wouldn't give any name she gave me a second thought if I were you. Would you?

Gobbel   If I were you?

Blunt   If you were him.

Gobbel   Not even if I was me!

Blunt   No, I'd just wipe it from my mind entirely and never even mention it! (*Pause.*) Now, Mr Conner, I don't want to speak out of turn here, but I think Mrs Conner should be resting, don't you? She looks very tired –

Balthasar   Oh – yes, dear – why don't you go back to bed for a while? I'll wake you when Carol comes, I promise.

Shandy   Carol! That was / the name they –

Gobbel *coughs loudly to cover him and* **Blunt** *all but manhandles* **Balthasar** *and* **Garson** *to the door.*

Blunt   No but I think you should go with her, don't you? Just to make sure she gets safely to bed –

Balthasar   Safely – ?

Blunt   You can never be sure, not in that state, believe me · – I mean – she could be straight out the back door, couldn't she?

Gobbel   Halfway down the road before you know it –

Blunt   Stark naked –

Balthasar   Stark naked?!

Blunt   Oh yes – !

Gobbel   Happens all the time.

Balthasar   Oh well, in that case, yes – will you excuse me, Reverend?

Shandy   Would you like me to come and sit with her?

Balthasar   Oh – well, if you –

Blunt   No! No, we have – matters to discuss – with the vicar, don't we?

Shandy   Do we?

Blunt   Yes, you know – community matters and – bereavement – coordination. That sort of thing.

He ushers **Balthasar** *and* **Garson** *out of the door.*

You go on and get her to bed. And make sure she gets to sleep.

Garson   Night, night, Daddy.

Blunt   Night – night.

He closes the door behind them.

Shandy   Bereavement coordination?

Blunt   Yes – haven't you heard of it?

Shandy   No, I haven't.

Gobbel   Well, it's definitely something that exists, isn't it?

Blunt   Absolutely.

Shandy   Is it, indeed. (*Pause.*) Well, I have a very pressing engagement so it'll have to be quick. (*Pause.*) Though, frankly, the only thing that's worrying me at the moment is Mrs Conner.

Blunt (*nods*)   I see. Take a note of that, Constable.

Gobbel   A real one?

Blunt   Yes, a real one! Now – what is it that's worrying you about Mr Conner?

Shandy   Well, I mean – he's just found out his only daughter's been killed on the motorway but frankly, he seems hardly at all.

Blunt (*nods*)   Hardly affected at all, yes, well now – you see, there may actually be a reason for that . . .

Shandy   Oh yes, undoubtedly. I've seen it before; total denial. The mind's defence mechanism. A refusal to even contemplate the truth.

Pause.

Blunt   Well, that's one possible reason . . .

Shandy   You think there's another?

Pause.

Like what?

Blunt   Well . . .

*Pause. He looks at **Gobbel** who urges him to tell.*

Well . . . the other possible reason could be that . . . well, that he might somehow think . . . that it's not actually his daughter that's dead but . . . well . . . maybe . . .

Shandy   Maybe what?

Pause.

Gobbel   His dog!

Shandy   His dog?!

Blunt (*nods*)   Miffy.

Pause.

Shandy   Ah, I see! You mean, not so much denial as transference? Yes . . . I've never encountered it but I suppose it's possible. Are you schooled in psychology, Officer?

Blunt   Well . . . I dabble.

Shandy   Oh yes, it's fascinating, don't you think?! If I had my life to live again, that's what I'd be; a psychiatrist. I love the way it all seems to fit together so easily. I mean, religion's all very well but it doesn't stand up to analysis, does it?
So you're saying that the mind acknowledges the event but substitutes the life lost for one of lesser importance?

Pause. **Blunt** *looks at* **Gobbel**. *Pause.*

Gobbel   He thinks it's his dog!

Shandy *looks confused.*

Shandy   Yes, but –

Gobbel *goes to him.*

Gobbel   You have to help us, Father, please!

Shandy   Help you?

Shandy *looks at* **Blunt**.

Blunt   You see, there was a small misunderstanding . . .

Gobbel   Large!

Blunt   A large misunderstanding and – well, it's a long story – but basically . . .

Gobbel   They think it's their dog!

Blunt   They think it's their dog.

Shandy (*pause*)   What, you mean – both of them? They both – (*Pause.*) You told them it was their dog?!

Gobbel } No!
Blunt } Yes!

Shandy   Well, which?

Gobbel   No!

Blunt   Well, yes, but – we didn't know that's what we were telling them when we told them –

Shandy   But when you found out you hadn't told them what you'd told them – didn't you tell them then?

Blunt   We've been trying!

Shandy   Trying?! You mean they don't know that their daughter's dead?!

Gobbel   His heart's like a paper bag!

Blunt   He has a heart condition –

Shandy   And so?

Gobbel   So if we tell him he'll die!

Shandy   You don't know that; you can't possibly!

Gobbel   He's got tiny pills.

Blunt (*nods*)   Very small pills.

Shandy   But you can't just not tell him that his daughter's dead!

Gobbel   SSSHHH!

Shandy (*whispering*)   You can't not tell him his –

Catches himself.

Oh for goodness sake! I've never heard such a thing in my life! You're police officers! You have to tell them!

Gobbel   But what about his heart?

Shandy   His heart's in God's hands, not yours! Why, it's nothing short of immoral!

Pause.

Shandy   Well?

Blunt   Now?

Shandy   Of course now! And not a moment longer!

Pause.

Blunt   It's actually not my turn . . .

Gobbel   I told them, fair and square!

Blunt   If you told them, why don't they know?

Gobbel   I don't know why they don't know but I know I told them!

Blunt   How can you tell someone something and then not know what they've been told?!

Gobbel   I don't know but I'll tell you this – !

Shandy   STOP THIS BICKERING RIGHT NOW!

Pause.

You're a disgrace to your office, both of you!

Gobbel (*pause*)   We don't have an office.

Blunt   We're going to tell him, Father, of course we are – We just need to tell him in the right way!

Shandy   In God's name, man – what right way is there to tell a man his child is dead?!

Gobbel   We could leave a note –

Shandy   A *NOTE*?!

Gobbel   Well, if you're so smart, you tell him!

Shandy   That's exactly what I'm going to do!

He heads for the door.

Blunt   No, wait – Father – let's just think about this a moment – !

They block the door.

Shandy   Stand away from the door.

Gobbel   The shock'll kill him!

Blunt   It'll be tantamount to murder!

Shandy   I'm warning you – You'll burn in Hell if you don't stand away from that door!

Gobbel   No we won't!

Shandy   You will; in the searing flames of Hell for all eternity!

Blunt   He's just trying to scare us! There's no such place!

Shandy   BE SURE, YOUR SIN SHALL FIND YOU OUT!

Gobbel   Stop shouting!

Shandy   ONLY THE TRUTH SHALL MAKE YOU FREE!

Blunt   You'll wake the neighbours!

Shandy   THE POWER OF CHRIST COMPELS YOU!

He tries to physically move them. There's a tussle; the three of them fall to the floor.

THE POWER OF CHRIST COMPELS YOU! THE POWER OF CHRIST COMPELS YOU!

Blunt *gets his hand over his mouth, muffling him.* **Shandy** *bites.*

Blunt   He's biting me!

Gobbel *tries to prise* **Shandy**'s *mouth open, to no avail.*

Blunt   Do something!

Shandy   THE POWER OF CHRIST COMPELS YOU!

Gobbel *takes out his truncheon –*

Shandy   THE POWER OF CHRIST COMP – !

– and whacks it over **Shandy**'s *head.*

Shandy *stands up.*

Shandy   What was that?

Gobbel *shows him the truncheon. Pause.* **Shandy** *nods.*

He goes limp and collapses.

Blunt *pulls free. The two of them stare at their handiwork. Pause.*

Blunt   What have you done?!

Pause. They both go to him. **Gobbel** *listens for his heart.*

Gobbel   There's no heartbeat!

Blunt   What?!

Gobbel   He's gone all hard!

Gobbel *thumps* **Shandy**'s *chest. It does, indeed, sound hard.*
Blunt *feels* **Shandy**'s *chest, listens. Pause. He reaches inside his
jacket and pulls out a Bible, which he throws at* **Gobbel.** **Blunt**
listens.

Blunt   It's all right – he's alive!

The door starts to open. It's **Balthasar.**

Gobbel   Blunt!

Blunt *intercepts him at the door.*

Balthasar   Are you all right in there?

Blunt   Yes, of course we're all right, why wouldn't we be all right? What makes you think we're not all right?

Balthasar   What was all that shouting?

Blunt   What shouting? I didn't hear any shouting –

Balthasar   Someone was shouting –

Blunt   How's Mrs Conner? Is she sleeping?

Gobbel *looks around, panicked. He spots a cupboard and drags* **Shandy** *towards it.*

Balthasar   Well, not sleeping exactly . . .

Blunt   No, not sleeping but – resting?

Balthasar   Resting, yes; more resting than sleeping –

Blunt   Resting, absolutely, well, after all, they do say that a rest is as good as a – as a sleep, don't they?

Balthasar   As good as – ? Oh, yes, I suppose they do – do they?

Blunt   They do, they do – they're always saying it, yes –

Gobbel *gets the cupboard door open but has some difficulty lifting the body in.*

Pause.

Balthasar   Do you think I could come in, at all?

Blunt   Come in? Oh, you mean – in here?

Balthasar   Yes, the uh –

Blunt   The living room?

Balthasar   Yes –

Blunt   Well, I mean, of course, I mean; it's your living room, isn't it? At the end of the day. And you can come and go as you please – Was that Mrs Conner?

Balthasar   What?

Blunt   Just then. I thought I heard something – sounded like Mrs Conner?

Balthasar   I didn't hear anything . . .

Blunt   Really? I could've sworn I heard something . . .

Balthasar   Is there something wrong, Officer?

Blunt   Wrong? No –

Balthasar   It's just you seem like you don't want me to come in –

Gobbel *gives* **Blunt** *the thumbs up.* **Blunt** *steps away from the door.*

Blunt   No, not at all. Come right in.

Balthasar *enters.* **Gobbel** *leans against the cupboard door, trying to look nonchalant.*

Balthasar   Where's Reverend Shandy?

Blunt   Oh – Reverend Shandy, yes; he had to go, didn't he?

Gobbel *nods.*

Blunt   He said he's sorry but – he had to go to see someone else who's also had a bereavement – but a much worse one than yours.

Balthasar   Oh no, really?

Blunt   Sadly, yes. He said he was sorry but seeing as it's only a dog he couldn't wait and that he hoped you had a very happy Christmas.

Balthasar   Oh, I see. Well, that was very nice of him to come anyway, wasn't it? I must say I wouldn't have expected so many people to be so caring about all this; it's really very kind of you all . . .

They nod guiltily.

I just don't know what's happened to Carol. She should have been here by now. You don't think anything's happened, do you?

Pause.

I suppose it's probably just the roads. I'd call her on her mobile phone thing but I'm always worried she'll get distracted and have an accident.

Blunt (*nods*)   No, you're absolutely right. Lot of accidents happen like that, don't they?

Gobbel   Yes, they don't, I mean, do.

Blunt   No, I wouldn't bother with that.

Balthasar   No. And you never get a good line anyway. I did give her a call earlier this evening and right in the middle of talking to her, it just cut off, just like that.

Pause.

Blunt   Cut off?

Balthasar   Cut off. No – there was a terrible noise, like an explosion almost – and then it just cut off, just like that. Cut off dead.

Pause. **Gobbel** *totters slightly*.

Gobbel   Blunt – I feel a bit funny . . .

Balthasar   Are you all right, Officer?

Gobbel *totters towards* **Blunt**.

Blunt   He's fine, he's just a little – claustrophobic. Why don't you have a seat, Constable? I'll take over here.

Blunt *takes his place by the wardrobe, grins at* **Balthasar**.

Balthasar   Now, where are my manners? I didn't get you that drink I promised, did I? What was it you were having again?

Gobbel   Brandy!

Balthasar   Brandy, was it?

Blunt   No! Something from the fridge.

Balthasar   Something from – ?

Blunt   Something cold, from the fridge.

Gobbel   Can't I have a brandy?

Blunt   Is the brandy in here?

Balthasar   Yes, it's –

Blunt   Then no; something from the fridge.

Gobbel   Why can't I have the brandy?

Blunt   Because it would be *good* – for Balthasar to *go* – and get us something from the *fridge*.

Pause. **Gobbel** *twigs.*

Gobbel   *Ohhh . . . !*

Balthasar   I'm not sure what there is in the fridge . . .

Blunt   Whatever there is will be just fine.

Pause. They stare at him.

Balthasar   Yes, all right, I'll . . . go to the fridge.

Smiling inanely, they wait for him to go. As soon as he's gone, they leap into life.

Blunt   We've got to get the vicar out of here before he comes round!

Gobbel   He killed her, Blunt! Did you hear him? He phoned her up and she got distracted and that's why she's dead!

Blunt   It could be worse.

Gobbel   How could it be worse?!

Blunt   She could be us! Now come and give me a hand!

Gobbel *drags himself up from the sofa.*

The small yap of a dog.

They both freeze. **Blunt** *turns to look at* **Gobbel**.

Pause.

Blunt   That's not funny.

Gobbel   I know.

Blunt   Making that noise.

Gobbel   I didn't.

Again, the yapping of a dog.

Pause.

They both turn, horrified, to look at the window. They run to the window and look out into the yard. The dog growls and yaps at them.

Blunt/Gobbel   Miffy!

They try to quiet it down: Shoo! Go away! etc.

Gobbel   What are we going to do?!

Blunt   Get rid of it!

Gobbel   Get rid of it?!

Blunt   Chase it away!

Gobbel   Chase it away how?!

Blunt   I don't know – throw a stick for it or something!

Gobbel   Me?!

Blunt   Oh, don't start that! Just get it away from here before they hear it!

Gobbel   How do I get out there?

Blunt   This way!

Gobbel *follows him to the door, but* **Blunt** *stops.*

Blunt   It's Balthasar! Quick – !

They run back to the window. **Blunt** *opens it, the yapping getting louder, and hurries* **Gobbel** *out.*

Gobbel   Blunt?

Blunt   What?!

Gobbel   I'm scared of dogs!

Blunt   It's a chihuahua!

Gobbel   I'm scared of them too!

Blunt   Just get out of there!

Gobbel   But how do I get (back in)?!

Blunt *shuts the window, just as* **Balthasar** *comes in.*

Balthasar   Now there's only one – Ah, there you are – now I'm afraid there's only one lager, but there's a bottle of cider if you'd care for a glass of that instead?

Blunt   That'd be dog.

Balthasar   Dog?

Blunt   Dog?!

Balthasar   Did you say dog?

Blunt   Dog? Why would I say dog? No, I said – fine. Cider would be fine. Thank you.

The sound of the dog yapping.

Balthasar   What was that?

Blunt   What?

Balthasar   Barking – outside . . .

The dog yaps and growls.

There! Didn't you hear it?

Pause. **Blunt** *shakes his head, feebly.*

It's there, behind you, at the window – !

Balthasar *starts towards the window.* **Blunt** *blocks him.*

Blunt   All right, Mr Conner, you're right; there is a barking noise.

Balthasar   There is, isn't there?

Blunt   Yes, but it's not a dog –

Balthasar   It's not?

Blunt   No, it's – children.

Balthasar   Oh – children?

Blunt   Yes – cruel, awful, delinquent children who think it's funny to make noises like a dog just to upset you!

Balthasar   Really? Doesn't sound like children . . .

Blunt   No, it's hard to believe, isn't it? But it is.

He turns back to the window.

This your idea of a joke, is it?! This your sick, twisted idea of a joke?! Taunting an old couple in their grief?! You sick and twisted little – delinquents!

He turns back to **Balthasar***.*

Now, Mr Conner, don't you worry yourself – my colleague is out there as we speak, getting rid of them. I'm just sorry you had to hear it.

Balthasar   Oh, well, yes, I suppose that's . . . children, you say?

There's a terrible sound of dog yapping and growling and shrieks from **Gobbel***.*

Goodness!

Blunt *looks out the window. He starts gesticulating to* **Gobbel***. More noise.*

Balthasar   What's going on out there?!

Balthasar *approaches the window again.*

Blunt   No, now, Mr Conner, I must insist that you stay back – for your own safety. My colleague has everything in hand.

Yaps, shrieks, the clatter of dustbins. Pause.

I wonder if I could bother you for that cider you so kindly offered?

Balthasar   Oh yes – certainly –

A clatter. The yelping stops.

Do you think he's (all right) – ?

Blunt   CIDER! (*Pause.*) Please. Would be nice. Thank you.

Balthasar   Yes, of course.

Balthasar *exits.*

Blunt *opens the window and* **Gobbel** *climbs back in, looking scratched and beat up and traumatised.*

Blunt   What were you doing?!

Gobbel   It went for me!

Blunt   Did you get rid of it?

Gobbel   I was throwing sticks for it but it just kept staring at me with its teeth out and slavers coming out its mouth and I bent down and it just went for me, right at my face, all fur and teeth and claws!

Blunt   Yes, but it's gone?

Gobbel   Sort of.

Blunt   What do you mean, sort of? You mean it might come back?

Gobbel   No – that's not what I mean! That's not what I mean at all!

Pause.

Blunt   What have you done?

Gobbel   I had no choice! It came right at me! Look at my hands! They're torn to shreds!

Pause.

It was trying to bite my face, I swear! I had to defend myself, didn't I? So I grabbed it by the back of the neck – like they do on *Pet Rescue* except –

Blunt   Except what?

Gobbel   Except I didn't rescue it!

Pause.

Blunt   What are you saying?

Pause. **Gobbel** *lifts his helmet. Under it is a dead dog.*

It's dead!

Gobbel   I know!

Blunt   You've killed it!

Gobbel   It was it or me, I swear!

Blunt   But you can't keep it there!

Gobbel   I know, but I couldn't think! I was frightened someone might see me! What am I going to do?! I'm a murderer! Blunt – I'm a dog murderer!

Blunt   Never mind that; we've got to get rid of it!

Gobbel   I want to bury it! I have to take it somewhere and give it a decent burial.

Blunt   Don't be ridiculous!

Gobbel   You don't understand! I've killed a dog! But I did it for him, Blunt! I did it to save Beelzebub, didn't I? It was the right thing to do, wasn't it?

Blunt   Yes, yes, whatever – just get the bloody thing out of here, quick!

Gobbel   But what'll I do with it?!

Blunt   I don't know, do I? Throw it in the bin or over the fence or something –

Gobbel   The fence?

Blunt *pushes* **Gobbel** *towards the door.*

Blunt   Put it in a cab and send it to the theatre! Anything, just for God's sake get it –

Balthasar *comes in just as they're going out.*

Balthasar   Well, they're nice and cold anyway, that's for –

Blunt *and* **Gobbel** *do an immediate about-turn.*

Blunt   That's it, just walk, keep walking –

Balthasar   Are you all right, Officer?

Gobbel   No!

Blunt   He's fine, just a spot of cramp, isn't it?

Gobbel *nods, trying to keep his helmet balanced.*

Blunt   Adrenalin, you see, from all that fighting crime. Causes the muscles to lactate. So the best thing is to walk around for a while. There we go – better now?

Balthasar *hands* **Blunt** *the drinks.*

Blunt   Thank you very much.

Gobbel   Thank you.

Balthasar   You saw the children off then?

Gobbel   Eh?

Blunt   Yes, yes, it's all taken care of.

Balthasar   It's remarkable really; I could've sworn it was an actual dog.

Blunt   Yes, I know, well, that's kids these days; they have an amazing capacity for – imitating animals, don't they?

Gobbel   Do they?

Blunt   Yes, they do.

Balthasar   Well, yes, but it's just that it sounded so like –

Blunt   Miffy?! Oh, really, Mr Conner, please! Sounded like Miffy!

Gobbel   Ludicrous!

Blunt   Next you'll be saying she's alive!

Gobbel   Alive!

Blunt   Have you heard of such a thing!?

Gobbel   The very idea of it!

Blunt   What on earth made you think it was Miffy?!

Balthasar   Well, I *didn't* think it was Miffy . . .

Blunt   Oh – you didn't?

Balthasar   No, goodness, no – it sounded like a *small* dog –

Gobbel   A chihuahua!

Balthasar   Yes, exactly. Nothing like Miffy. Miffy was a Labrador.

The doorbell rings. **Blunt** *and* **Gobbel** *freeze.*

Now that *must* be Carol now! Seven hours that's taken from Bristol to here. Maybe you can be on your way at last.

Balthasar *exits.*

Pause. **Blunt** *looks at* **Gobbel**.

Blunt   A Labrador.

Gobbel   How was I to know?! It was you that told me to get rid of it!

Pause.

Blunt   D'you know – there are some people . . . who are so consistently predictable . . . that they actually end up unpredictable again.

Pause.

Gobbel   Maybe it's for the best anyway.

Blunt   For the best?! What, that you've killed a chihuahua?! How can that be for the best? How can any of this be for the best?!

Gobbel   Well, you'd never get a Labrador under a helmet, would you?

Blunt (*pause*)   Look – just get rid of it anyway!

Blunt *goes to listen at the door.*

Gobbel   But where though?!

Blunt   Anywhere it can't be found!

Gobbel   How am I going to find somewhere that can't be found?!

Blunt   Because it's the same place they keep your brain!

He opens the door a bit and recoils in fright.

A young girl enters.

Blunt   Who are you?

Carol (*pause*)   Carol.

Pause. **Blunt** *and* **Gobbel** *look at each other.*

Blunt   Carol?!

Gobbel   But you're – ?

Blunt   But we –

Gobbel   Supposed to be . . .

Blunt   Thought you were . . .

They approach her slowly, in awe. She backs away.

Carol   Supposed to be what? Thought I was what?

Gobbel *touches her.*

Carol   Get off me!

Gobbel   She's real, Blunt! She's really real!

Carol   What d'you mean, I'm real? Course I'm real!

Blunt   But what about the accident?

Carol   What accident?

Gobbel   The one that killed you!

Carol   The one that killed me?!

Blunt   You didn't have an accident? On the way here?

Gobbel   Not even a small one?

Girl   I'm going to have a big one any minute, you keep on acting so creepy!

Gobbel   They must've made a mistake, at the station, like I said!

Blunt   But you're not thirty-four . . . ?!

Carol   No, I'm nineteen. Nearly.

Blunt   So you're eighteen?

Carol   Yeah. (*Pause.*) Nearly.

Blunt   They said she was thirty-four . . . ?

Gobbel   So?! It doesn't matter! All that matters is she's here and she's safe and it was all a big mistake and Blunderbuss isn't going to die and Christmas isn't ruined and we're saved, Blunt!

Gobbel   We've got to tell Bulbusar the good news!

Blunt   We haven't told him the bad news yet!

Gobbel   We can tell him that later!

Blunt   Carol, forgive us – this must all sound a bit odd. Where's your father?

Carol (*shrugs*)   Don't know. Don't care either.

Blunt (*pause*)   Is he bringing your stuff in?

Carol   I don't have any stuff, honest?

Blunt   No, but from the car –

Carol (*pause*)   I just want to get through the back. Can I go through?

Blunt   Oh – to see your mother?

Carol   Is she here?

Pause.

Blunt   There's something wrong here somewhere.

Balthasar *enters.*

Balthasar   Ah, there you are – have you looked out the back?

Carol   Not yet, no –

Balthasar   Oh well, anyway, he's not in the garage, far as I can see, but if you go through the back there, to the kitchen, that'll get you into the yard –

Carol   Through there?

Balthasar   Straight through, yes.

Eyeing them suspiciously, **Carol** *leaves.*

Blunt   That's Carol?

Balthasar   I know, it's odd, isn't it? There's me waiting for Carol and a Carol arrives, but the wrong one. I mean, what are the odds on that?

Pause. **Blunt** *looks at* **Gobbel***, who's deflated.*

Blunt   Astronomical.

Gobbel *looks heavenwards.*

Balthasar   That's not all; remember I said that sounded like a small dog and you said a chihuahua? Well, that's what she's lost – a chihuahua. I know you said it was children but maybe there was a dog as well, I don't know; anyway, she's been looking for it all night. Just got it yesterday, for Christmas, poor thing, so I said have a look. Not a good day for dogs all round, is it?

He looks out the window. He gesticulates at the girl in the yard.

I don't think it's there, if it ever was. Oh dear.

Pause. He gestures for her to come back round.

Still doesn't explain what's happened to my Carol. It's really getting late now. You don't think anything's happened, do you, Officer? You'd have heard, wouldn't you?

They can only hang their heads.

Oh dear, where's she going? That's not the way . . .

Balthasar *shuffles over to the door. Exits.*

Blunt   This is like some kind of nightmare!

Gobbel *takes off his helmet and looks inside.*

Gobbel   She just got it, Blunt! It was a Christmas present! It was a Christmas present and we killed it!

Blunt   'We' killed it?!

Unbeknown to them, **Carol** *– confused about where she is – has arrived at the window.*

Gobbel   I killed it, you killed it, what's the difference?! All that matters is the poor thing's killed!

He pulls it out of the helmet in one gesture, holding it aloft. **Carol** *sees this and screams.*

Shocked, **Blunt** *and* **Gobbel** *stare at her.*

She passes out on the spot.

Gobbel   Oh my God, she's dead!

Blunt   What do you mean, dead?!

Gobbel   Her heart's given out!

Blunt   Don't talk rubbish! She's just fainted! Quickly – get her inside!

Gobbel *throws down the dead dog and heads out the hallway door.*

Blunt   Don't leave that there! (*Meaning the dog.*)

But **Gobbel** *rushes back in.*

Gobbel   Balderdash!

Panicked, **Blunt** *stuffs the dog into his own helmet and puts it on. He rushes past* **Gobbel** *to the door.*

Blunt   Bring her in through the window – I'll stall him!

The door starts to open –

Balthasar (*off*)   I can't seem to –

Blunt *stops the door.*

Gobbel *opens the window and climbs out, shutting it behind him.*

Blunt   Can't seem to what?

Balthasar (*pause*)   I can't seem to find the young lady.

Gobbel *has lifted* **Carol** *up but now he can't get back in the window.*

Balthasar   Is she in there with you at all?

Blunt   With me?

Gobbel *knocks on the window.* **Blunt** *sees him and groans.*

Blunt   No, unfortunately not.

Balthasar   Oh . . .

Pause.

Is it possible to come in at all?

Pause.

Blunt   Oh, wait a minute – I just saw her!

Balthasar   Did you?

Blunt   She's on her way to the back door! You better go and let her in!

Balthasar   Oh no, I left it open for her . . .

Blunt   Are you sure?

Balthasar   Am I – ? Well, I think so, yes . . .

Blunt   But I mean – with all due respect – you are getting on a bit; memory's probably not what it used to be –

Pause.

Balthasar   I don't think it's too bad –

Blunt   Well, that's not what you told me.

Balthasar   When?

Blunt   See what I mean? (*Pause.*) Better make sure.

Balthasar (*pause*)   Oh, well – I suppose . . .

Pause. **Blunt** *checks he's going then rushes to the window, opens it.*

Blunt   Quickly!

Between the two of them they manhandle **Carol** *through the window.*

Gobbel *collapses, exhausted.* **Blunt** *struggles with her body.*

Gobbel   I can't go on with this, Blunt!

Blunt   Get up and help me!

Gobbel   Help you with what?

Blunt   Help me hide her!

Gobbel *takes her legs and backs towards the wardrobe.*

Blunt   Not there!

Gobbel   Not there?!

Blunt   We can't put her in with the vicar!

Gobbel   Where then?!

Blunt   Over here! Quickly!

They carry her over to the chest and manage to put her in. **Blunt** *closes the lid.*

Gobbel   Can she breathe in there?

Blunt   It's mahogany, not tupperware! Right – now what?

The doorbell goes and they shriek with surprise.

Gobbel   Who's that?!

Blunt   How should I know?!

Balthasar *enters.*

Balthasar   Was that the doorbell again?

They nod, yes – weary with it.

I don't know what happened to that girl – she was going to the back door, you say? Just seems to have disappeared.

The doorbell goes again.

That surely must be Carol now; I'm terribly sorry about all this.

Balthasar *exits.*

Blunt   Right – we've got to take control of this situation! We've been at the mercy of events too long! Now's the time to employ every facet of our training!

Gobbel   Right!

Blunt   Now! First – aims, in no particular order; revive child, remove vicar, dispose of dog – what have I missed?

Pause.

There's something else we were meant to do; but what was it?

Gobbel   Something else we were meant to do . . .

Pause.

Blunt   Never mind, it'll come back to me; you get rid of the dog.

Gobbel   Right –

He picks up his helmet and heads towards the hall. He stops in his tracks –

Blunt!

Blunt   What?!

Gobbel   It's gone!

Blunt   What?!

Gobbel   The chihuahua – it's gone!

Blunt   How can it be gone?!

Gobbel   Maybe it's a zombie, Blunt! A zombie chihuahua!

Blunt   No, wait – I've got it under here!

Gobbel   What's it doing under there?!

Blunt   Not bloody much! Here –

He starts to take it off. Voices behind the door.

Gobbel   Blunt!

Blunt *hurriedly puts it back on.*

Balthasar *enters.*

Balthasar   No, no, not at all, I'm happy to help in any way I can . . . Ah, Officers, allow me to introduce Miss . . .

To their horror, it's **Gronya**.

Gronya   That's Mrs.

Balthasar   Oh, I beg your pardon – Miss Gronya –

Gronya   Just Gronya.

Balthasar   She says there's some sort of child molester in the area –

Blunt   We know.

Balthasar   Oh well – there you go. Who is it?

Blunt   No, we know what she's looking for –

Gronya   We've already met.

Balthasar   Oh, really, have you?

Gronya   Surprised you're still here.

Gobbel   So are we.

Pause. She looks up at the sash.

Gronya   Oh. (*Pause.*) So this is . . . ?

Blunt (*nods*)   Mr Conner.

Gronya   Oh, right, well – it's nothing for you to worry about. Got enough on your plate. I'm just asking people to keep their eyes open, let us know if you see or hear anything suspicious.

Balthasar   Oh, yes, well, of course I will – can't be having that sort of thing going on, can we?

Gronya   No. (*Pause.*) Well – I'll be on my way then.

She starts for the door. Stops.

I just want to say – I'm very sorry to hear about your loss.

Balthasar   About my – ? Oh, yes, well – thank you very much. I'm a little surprise you have heard about it, to be honest . . .

Gronya   It's a terrible thing, that sort of . . . thing.

Balthasar   Oh well, yes, of course, it is; but she had a fair innings, I think.

Gronya (*pause*)   Did she?

Blunt   I think it's probably best to let Mr Conner rest now.

Gronya   Shut it a minute – what do you mean, she had a fair innings?

Balthasar   Well, eight or nine years; that's not too bad, is it?

Gronya   Eight or nine?!

Balthasar   Yes, I think so, thereabouts. Why?

Gronya   Well – it's not my business, really; I just wouldn't say eight or nine was a fair innings . . .

Balthasar   No, but in dog years, what's that?

Gronya   Dog years?

Balthasar   Seven, is it, or is that cats? No, cats are shorter – it's seven so that's –

Gronya   But what's dog years got to do with your daughter?

Balthasar   My daughter? Nothing . . .

Blunt and **Gobbel** *are clutching their faces.*

Gronya   So who is it that died?

Balthasar   Who – ? Oh, Miffy was her name; my wife's dog. Labrador. Beautiful eyes, very sad.

Gronya *nods her head.*

Gronya   Oh very good. Very good. Everything worked out perfect; everything except the cover story. He thinks it's his dog, you say it's his daughter. I had you pegged as nellies from the off and I was bang on the money.

Pause.

Gobbel   What's she talking about?

Blunt   I don't know. What are you talking about?

She looks at **Balthasar**, *nodding.*

Gronya   So this is him, is it? The snake in the grass. It's always the same – look like butter wouldn't melt. The Mother Superior looked like that; like the kindest, frailest old granny you'd ever hope to have. But underneath the habit – a twisted, pie-fingering old Dyke.

Gobbel   What's a dyke?

Balthasar   I think I've missed something, have I? . . .

Gronya   You're going to be missing a whole lot more by the end of the night.

Blunt   You can't be serious – !

Gronya   You stay where you are, Dibble.

She takes out a mobile phone, dials.

Gobbel   What's going on?

Blunt   She thinks he's the paedophile!

Balthasar   I'm sorry, she thinks I'm the what?

Blunt   Look, you've got this all wrong –

Gronya   I said STAY WHERE YOU ARE!!
(*Into phone.*) Ballbreaker One here, who's that?
All right, well I've located King Rat. Repeat – I have located King Rat. And a couple of collaborators, too.
Yup; red-handed where are you?
Right, well, position's secure for now but you should get over pronto. It's Hobb Street.
What's the number here?

Blunt   Thirty-seven.

Gobbel   Fifty-eight, isn't it?

Gronya   Fifty-eight. Yeah.
And Barry – bring the toolkit.

She shuts off the phone.

Gobbel   Why's she bringing a toolkit?

Blunt   Well, it's not to do the plumbing, is it?!

Gronya   It is, actually.

Gobbel   Well, that's a relief!

Gronya   *Yours!*

Gobbel   That's not a relief.

Blunt   Now, just look here a minute – first of all, this is a total misunderstanding. Mr Conner isn't a paedophile and we're not here to smuggle him out. Just give me a chance to explain –

Gronya   Go ahead.

Blunt   No, not here – alone.

Gronya   Bollocks, no. Explain or don't. Explain why I've lived here all me life and never once clapped eyes on your man here.

Blunt   I don't know – sometimes people just don't see each other. And anyway, what are you suggesting?

Gronya   That it's all a sham. That he's been here five years tops.

Blunt   Well, that's just ridiculous!

Gronya   Prove it.

Blunt   Prove it?

Gronya   If you can.

Blunt   Of course I can! There must be a hundred ways to prove it; it's just choosing one . . .

The door opens. It's **Garson**.

Garson   What's going on here?

Blunt   Ah – the very person!

Gronya   Who's this?

Blunt   This – happens to be *Mrs Conner*!

Gobbel   Mr Conner's wife.

Blunt   Now – Mrs Conner – perhaps you could tell this lady how long you and Balthasar have been married?

She looks at them fearfully.

Garson   Well . . . about . . .

Pause. She looks at **Gronya**.

Gronya   It's all right. Just tell the truth.

Blunt   Yes – that's all we want; the truth.

Garson *goes to* **Gronya**.

Garson   I don't know who he is! They say he's here to help me but I don't trust him! Who is he?!

Blunt   No, you don't understand – !

Gronya   Shut it! This man's not your husband?

Garson   I don't have a husband!

Gronya   What have you sick bastards been up to?!

Blunt   You don't understand –

Groyna   Forcing an old woman into helping you with your sick charade? No, I don't understand! And I hope I never do!

Garson   Can't they just take him away? I'm scared!

Gronya   It's all right, love – you're safe now –

Blunt   She thinks she's on a boat!

Gronya   She what?

Blunt   She thinks she's on a boat! She's in shock or senile or something but she thinks she's on a boat, doesn't she?

Gobbel (*nods*)   She thinks I'm a Viscount!

Gronya   I don't care if she thinks you're a fucking Garibaldi! 'He's' not her husband!

Blunt   She thinks she's on a cruise liner! Mrs Conner, tell her! You're on a ship, aren't you?

Garson   A ship . . . ?

Blunt   Yes – I'm the Captain, remember?

Gronya   The Captain . . . ?

Gobbel   He's always in the altogether.

Gronya   He's what?

Gobbel   You know – Starkers. In his cabin.

Gronya   Starkers in his cabin?!

Gobbel   When the girls go in!

Gronya   Girls?!

Blunt   You're not helping –

Gobbel   No, but it's all right, though; they're all backwards.

Gronya   Starkers in his cabin with backward girls?! That's the most perverted thing I ever heard!

Blunt   Not *me*!

Gronya   Oh, you think that's all right, do you?! Showing your diddlestick to retarded young girls?

Blunt   No, look – Ask her what year it is. Ask her what year she thinks it is!

Gronya   What year is it? Can you hear me? D'you know what year it is?

Pause. She straightens.

Garson   Of course I know what year it is!

Gronya   Of course she knows what year it is!

Garson   It's 1961.

Gronya   It's Nineteen – it's what?

Garson   Martha, you know, if you're going to keep drinking that stuff, I suggest you invest in a diary. At least you'd keep track of the days.

Gronya   Did you call me Martha?

Garson   Oh, really! I don't see why you're in such a state! Anyone'd think it was you that'd just been publicly humiliated.

Blunt (*to* **Balthasar**)   What's she talking about?

Balthasar   I've really no idea! Garson, dear, what are you talking about? What's happening to you?

Pause. She hugs him.

Garson   Oh, Daddy! What am I going to do? How can I ever show my face again?

Gronya   He's her father?

Blunt   Course he's not! How could he be her father?

Gobbel   Maybe he had her at sixteen!

Gronya   He what?

Garson *turns to face* **Gobbel**.

Garson   You!

Gobbel   Me?

She advances on him, pointing.

Garson   How dare you show your face here! After what you've done! You absolute beast!

Gobbel   What have I done?

Garson   Don't you dare! Don't you dare act the innocent with me, Balthasar Conner!

Gobbel   *Who*?

Gronya (*pointing at* **Balthasar**)   I thought he was Balthasar?

Blunt   He is!

Balthasar   I am!

Garson   How could you do that to me?! How could you disgrace me like that, in front of all those people?!

Gobbel   All what people?

Garson   Our families, our friends, the vicar; all of them! Standing there in that stupid wedding dress, like an idiot!

Gronya   Wedding dress?

Gobbel   I'm not wearing a wedding dress!

Blunt   No, wait – she thinks she's at a wedding!

Gronya   He stood her up! Is that what you're saying? He stood you up at your wedding?

Garson   Oh, Martha, you know damn well he did!

Gobbel   I didn't stand anyone up!

Blunt   Not you – she thinks you're Balthasar!

Gobbel   So who's Bulbousear?

Blunt   He's her father!

Gobbel   So who's me?

Blunt   You're not here!

Gobbel   Where am I then?!

Blunt   On the slow boat to Cairo – how should I know?!

Garson (*to* **Blunt**)   And you're no better!

Blunt   Me?!

Garson   Yes, you – messenger boy! If you were a man instead of his spineless stooge, you'd have refused to bring that letter and made him come to the church in person!

Blunt   Now hold on a moment – !

Gronya   What letter?

Blunt   I'm nobody's stooge, and least of all his!

Gobbel (*points at* **Balthasar**)   His!

Blunt   Or his or – (anyone's)

Gronya   Shut it, the pair of you!
What did it say, this letter?

Garson   What did it say? (*Pause.*) That he couldn't go through with the wedding. That he had never truly loved me. That his heart was with another.

Gobbel   Another what?

Gronya   Another girl, you dunce!

Blunt   Who, though?

Garson   Someone he could never have. (*Pause.*) He said he was sorry that he couldn't tell me to my face. He said he was sorry he had let it come to this. He said he was sorry – but that that . . . was that.

They all stare at **Balthasar**.

Gronya   Is that what you did?

Balthasar   No, I . . .

Why are you telling them this?

Garson *turns to face* **Balthasar**.

Garson   Because you make me sick, that's why! Nice old Balthasar! Gentle old Balthasar! What's he doing with that

grumpy old bag? She cares more about that dog than him.
He really deserves better. Such a gentleman. So patient.
And so very, very kind!

She addresses the others.

So what do you think of that? Standing up your bride on
her wedding day? Not very kind, is it? In fact, most people
would say it was positively cruel. Wouldn't you agree,
Officers? Wouldn't you say that it was positively cruel?

Pause.

Gobbel } Sounds fairly cruel to me . . .
Blunt } I'd say that was cruel, yes . . .

Garson   Yes. (*Pause.*) Well, so would my husband. Which
is why he arrived at the church in good time, with not a hair
out of place, and stood there before God, with his kind smile
and eyes, and married a young woman that he didn't love
and never would.

Pause.

Gobbel   So who was she?

Balthasar   That's not fair, Garson. They were different
days. I did what I thought was right.

Garson   Horseshit! You did what would cause the least
embarrassment, the least fuss – !

Balthasar   The least hurt –

Garson   Balls! It was nothing to do with not hurting me!
It was all about you; about how you would look, to me, to
the neighbours, about how your damned family would look!
You threw away both our lives and for what?! For the sake
of appearances!

Pause.

Gronya   So he is your husband, then?

Garson   Yes. He's my husband. For better or for worse.

Gronya   Right. So he's not the dirty paedo?

Garson   Oh, get a life!

Garson *exits. Pause.*

Balthasar   I'm terribly sorry about all that. Dreadfully embarrassing. I don't know what's come over her . . . these days.

Blunt   No, well, you know . . . Women, eh?

Gobbel   Yeah – women!

Gronya   You're a bunch of wallies, the lot of you! She's saying her husband doesn't love her; d'you know what that's like?

Gobbel   I do, actually!

Balthasar   But I do, though. Since our daughter was born, anyway. I've loved her ever since.

Gobbel   So it wasn't a total waste, was it? Cos at least you've got your daughter.

Balthasar   Yes, that's right; we've got Carol. She's all we ever had.

Gronya   But that's good, listen – I'd have given anything for two parents that loved me – I mean, like, in a non-sexual way –

Gobbel   Me too!

Gronya   Were you abused as a child?

Gobbel   I wish!

Gronya   You what?!

Her mobile phone rings. She takes it.

Gronya   Ballbreaker One?
Yeah, I'm still here –
When was this?
So who is it?

You're joking – !
No, it's just bleedin' typical, isn't it?
But we don't have a name?
Well, it narrows the field, doesn't it?

Pause. She looks at **Blunt**.

No. I was wrong about that. Better just return to base and
we can go from there.
Right.

She shuts it. To all:

Well – looks like you're off the hook.

Blunt   How's that then?

Gronya   We got some new information.

Blunt   Like what?

Gronya   Wouldn't you like to know!

Blunt   Hold on a moment – You can't just go taking the
law into your own hands! If you know something about a
criminal in the area, you've got to tell us, hasn't she?

Gobbel   Or at least tell the police.

Blunt   Or at least – We 'are' the bloody police!

Gobbel   'Language'.

Blunt   Never mind language; someone could end up dead!

Gobbel   D'you reckon?

Gronya   Not someone; a crawling, slimy nonce!

Blunt   Balthasar – tell her!

Balthasar   Tell her what?

Blunt   Tell her not to do it!

Balthasar   You know, he's right, dear. I can't see what
good it'll do. Whoever this monster is, he'll have to answer
to God.

Gronya   Answer to God?! That's a bloody laugh! He's the biggest nonce of the lot!

Gobbel   God's a nonce?

Balthasar   Oh now, you shouldn't say things like that . . .

Gronya   You don't know what you're talking about, old man! I was brought up by the so-called Sisters of Mercy and I'll say what I bleedin' well like!

Balthasar   No, but the Church does a lot of good work . . .

Gronya   Good work? Good bleeding work? Well, here's how much you know; he's a vicar!

Blunt   Who is?

She waves her mobile phone.

Gronya   The chicken-handler! The kiddie-fiddler! He's a bloody vicar, surprise surprise! He's probably at the church right now, having his bell rung! That's how much you know, you old FOOL!

She goes to the door but **Gobbel** *has blocked it.*

Gobbel   No – we won't let you do it!!

Blunt   What are you doing?

Gronya   Get out of my way, copper!

Gobbel   She's going to kill the vicar!

Blunt   No, let her go!

Gobbel   But we can't let her kill someone – remember what the sarge said; don't let people – kill – other people.

Gronya   I'm going to count to three –

Blunt   Constable – let her go!

Gobbel   But it's tenterhook to murder!

Gronya   ONE!

Blunt   I'm sure the vicar is somewhere safe!

He indicates the cupboard.

Gronya   TWO!

Blunt   I'm sure he's locked away somewhere safe!

Gobbel   Are you going to three or five?

Gronya   THREE!

Pause.

Right!

She grabs him by the lapels.

Gobbel   Was that the three there?

Gronya   That was the three – and now you're out!

She retracts her fist to punch him and then there are three thumps from inside the wardrobe.

Pause. Everyone freezes.

Gronya   What was that?

Blunt *stamps his foot three times.*

Blunt   One, two, three!

Another three thumps from inside the wardrobe, and **Shandy***'s voice –*

Shandy   Somebody open this door!

Gobbel   Ohhhh! *Now* I get you: somewhere safe!

Blunt   You idiot!

Gronya *slowly approaches the wardrobe. She opens the door and* **Shandy** *rolls out.*

Blunt   Reverend Shandy!

Shandy (*to* **Gronya**)   Who are you?!

Gronya   Who am I?!

Shandy *sees* **Blunt** *and* **Gobbel**.

Shandy   You! You'll pay for this! How dare you treat me this way?!

Blunt (*pause*)   Reverend! What are you doing in the cupboard?!

Shandy   Don't give me that! You know exactly why I was in the cupboard!

Gronya   And why's that?

Shandy   Because they put me in it! Hit me over the head and stuffed me in!

Gronya   Did they now?!

Shandy   It's nothing short of an outrage!

Gronya (*to* **Balthasar**)   Did you know he was in there?

Balthasar   No, I thought he'd gone!

Gronya   What do you mean, gone?

Balthasar   Well, I don't know – he came round to offer his condolences on Miffy dying (and then) –

Shandy   Miffy – that's right, the dog!

Gronya *grabs* **Shandy**.

Gronya   Shut it! (*To* **Balthasar**.) Go on.

Balthasar   Well, that's it, really – I took my wife through to her bed – and the Reverend stayed here because the officers wanted to talk to him about something –

Gronya   Did they now?

Shandy   What's going on here! Unhand me this instant!

Gronya   I'll un'cock' you, you don't shut up! Now sit down and don't move!

She pushes **Shandy** *towards the couch. She walks over to* **Blunt** *and* **Gobbel**.

Well, now. Seems I underestimated you boys. Have to get the paedo out of town but you can't turn up on his doorstep, can you, case one of us clocks you. So you come here on the pretence of telling them their cat's dead and arrange for the so-called Father to meet you here. Not bad. Almost even clever.

Shandy   Will someone please tell me what's going on here?

Gronya   Oh, listen to it squeal! What's going on is you've been rumbled, mate!

Shandy   I've been what?

Gronya   We're on to you! You've been caught!

Shandy   Caught by who?

Gobbel   The PAPS.

Shandy   Caught by the PAPS!

Gronya (*to* **Balthasar**)   All right, old man. I'm giving you the benefit of the doubt. Off you go and sit with your wife; and stay there till I tell you otherwise.

Balthasar   But – what are you going to do?

Gronya   I don't know yet. But I'll try not to stain the sofa.

Blunt/Gobbel   Stain the sofa?

Shandy   Stain the sofa with what?!

Gronya   On you go now.

She ushers **Balthasar** *out, shuts the door behind him. She opens her mobile.*

Shandy   This place is a madhouse!

Gronya   Ballbreaker one – where are you?
Well, turn around – I was right all along.
I'm looking at him right now.
Yeah, I know. Maybe there is a God after all.

Have we still got that tarpaulin in the back?
Good. We'll need it.

She closes the phone.

All right, Gary Glitter – let's have your togs off!

Gronya *takes* **Gobbel**'s *truncheon from his belt.*

Shandy   I beg your pardon?!

Gronya   Clothes. Off. Now!

Shandy   Over my dead body!

Gronya   Fair enough.

She whacks **Shandy** *over the head. As before, he stands up straight.*

Shandy   Did you just hit me with that truncheon?

Gronya   I believe I did.

Pause. He nods.

Shandy   Right.

He collapses, unconscious. **Gronya** *sets about undressing him.*

Blunt   Now *that* – is definitely illegal!

Gronya   So's playing the baby banjo. Now sit down or
you'll get the same. I'll deal with you two turncoats later.

She takes **Shandy**'s *jacket off.* **Shandy** *burbles, semi-conscious.*

Gobbel   Why's she taking his clothes off?

Blunt   Why are you taking his clothes off?

Gronya   It's Christmas, isn't it?

Blunt   So?

Gronya   So you pluck the turkey before you stuff it, don't
you?

Gobbel (*pause*)   Where'd you get a turkey from? I couldn't
get one anywhere . . .

Blunt   Shut up about the turkey!

Gronya   Up we get, Reverend.

She stands the semi-conscious reverend up, and starts to undo his trousers.

Shandy   Must we have cucumber again? It tastes of so very little.

Blunt   Look, you've got this all wrong, I swear! I know you've been told the paedophile is a vicar but there's no evidence to prove that Reverend Shandy's the one you're –

She pulls his trousers down. Surprisingly, **Shandy** *is wearing stockings, suspenders and little lacy panties.*

Gronya   Well – bloody – well!

Pause.

Blunt   All right, admittedly, that looks bad. But it doesn't mean he's a child molester!

Gronya   So what does it mean, then? A vicar wearing women's underwear?! What exactly does that mean?

Blunt   Well, it means that he's –

He looks desperately at **Gobbel**.

Gobbel   A woman!

Blunt   A woman?!

Gronya   He doesn't look like a woman.

Gobbel   You can talk!

Gronya   You what?

Blunt   No, what he means is that – he's not a woman – yet. But he wants to be.

Gronya   What are you talking about?!

Gobbel (*pause*)   He's a man trapped in a woman's body!

Blunt   No –

Gobbel   He's a *woman* trapped in a woman's body!

Blunt   No!

Gobbel   A man trapped in – ?

Blunt   He's a woman trapped in a *man's* body.

Gronya   And how d'you know this? Friend of yours, is he?

Blunt ⎰ No!
Gobbel ⎱ Yes!

Blunt   I mean, no, not so much a friend as . . .

Gobbel   A colleague!

Gronya   A colleague? What, so you're vicars, are you?

Blunt   No . . .

Gobbel   But neither's he!

Blunt   But neither's he!

Gronya   He's not a vicar?

Blunt   No, he's – he's –

Gobbel   He's a stripagram!

Gronya   Oh, he's a stripagram, is he?

Gobbel   We all are!

Gronya   You're all stripagrams, are you? Is that right, Reverend? You a stripagram, are you?

Shandy   Oh, yes please!

Gobbel   Yes; and that's why – we couldn't explain!

Blunt   Yes! Of course! That's why we couldn't explain! Because it's meant to be a surprise!

Gobbel   Because we're here – / for the daughter!

Blunt   For the daughter / exactly!

Gronya   What daughter?

Gobbel   The one that died!

Blunt   The one that didn't die – ! Mr and Mrs Conner's daughter –

Gobbel   Miffy –

Shandy   Carol!

Blunt   Carol, exactly – is coming home tonight, after a while away – and we've been hired to – strip. When she gets here, haven't we?

Gronya   Hired by who?

Pause.

Blunt   Well – by a friend of hers.

Gronya   Who?

Blunt   Who?

Gobbel   We don't know.

Blunt   That's right, we don't know.

Gronya   You don't know who hired you?

Blunt   Why would we? The agency just tells us where to go and that's where we go.

Gronya   And what agency's this?

Blunt   The agency we work for.

Gronya   Which is?

Pause.

Blunt   Stripper . . . vicars.

Gronya   Strippervicars?

They nod.

But you're not vicars.

Blunt   No, well, they don't just do vicars. That's just the name. They do all sorts – vicars, policemen –

Gobbel   That's us.

Blunt   Firemen . . .

Gobbel   Postmen . . .

Blunt   All sorts.

Gobbel   Taxi drivers –

Blunt   Yes, I think she's got the picture.

Pause.

Gronya   So let's say I was stupid enough to believe you –

Gobbel   Are you?

Gronya   No. But it still doesn't explain why he was in the cupboard.

Blunt   Ah, well, that's easy, isn't it?

Gobbel   Easy-peasy.

Pause.

Gronya   I'm waiting.

Blunt   You're not a very trusting person, are you?

Gronya   No, but I'm a very violent person if that's any incentive.

Blunt (*pause*)   Well, you see – it's all part of the surprise. It's what we call the – double surprise special. Yes, you see, the victim arrives – not the victim, I mean the um –

Gobbel   The deceased.

Blunt   The deceased – no! Not the deceased, the um – the client! Yes – that's what I mean, the client – the client arrives and we do, you know, our um . . . routine . . . and then they think that's it but then the doors open and out comes the vicar!

Gobbel And that's the second surprise!

Blunt Hence the name.

Gronya Which doesn't explain why you whacked him on the nut in the first.

Pause.

Gobbel That's the third surprise.

Gronya Is it now? (*Pause.*) So why didn't you tell me all this from the off?

Blunt Well, we couldn't, could we? I mean, for all we knew, you might've been the girl or one of her friends even. We'd never work again, would we?

Gronya *nods. Pause. She takes out her mobile and starts to dial.* **Blunt** *and* **Gobbel** *barely contain their relief.*

Blunt You're really making absolutely the right choice. If your friends come here, we'll all look stupid.

Gronya I'm not calling them.

Blunt Who are you calling?

Gronya My daughter.

She puts the phone to her ear. But we can hear a phone ringing somewhere, muffled.

Pause. It's coming from the chest.

Gronya *follows the sound to the chest. She flings it open.*

Gronya Carol?!

She drags the girl out of the chest. She's barely conscious.

Carol Mum . . . ?

Gronya What the bollocks are you doing in her?! What have these bastards done to you?!

Now she's really angry. She turns to **Blunt** *and* **Gobbel***, and advances on them.*

What the fucking SHITE is going on here?! What is my Carol doing in that thing?!

Blunt   Now there's no need for bad language –

Gronya   Bad fucking language? Bad fucking cunty arse fucking language? WHAT HAVE YOU DONE TO MY DAUGHTER?!

Blunt   Nothing, I swear!

Gronya   Has that pervert touched her?

Gobbel   She fainted!

Blunt   That's right, she fainted!

Gronya   She fainted?! Why did she faint?! Because the pervert molested her?!!

Carol   No, because they killed Chinkie!

Gronya   Chinkie the chihuahua? That we got you for your Christmas?

Carol   Yeah, he run away!

Gronya   How'd he get out the gift box?

Carol   He pissed it soft and ate his way out!

Gronya   I told you not to give him water, didn't I? So he run away?

Carol   And I went to look for him and the man said he was out there –

Gronya   What man?

Carol   The old cunt that lives here!

Gronya *slaps her.*

Gronya   Don't you swear, you cunt!

Carol   I didn't! But so he says he's out there, so I go through here and I go out there, but he's not there, these two cunts have killed him!

Gronya   Which two cunts?!

Carol   These two cunts!

Gronya *slaps her.*

Gronya   I said don't fucking swear!

Carol   I didn't!

Gronya   What's she talking about?! Did you kill my daughter's dog?!

They feign innocence.

Carol   He's under his hat!

Gronya   Under his hat?!

She points at **Gobbel**.

Carol   This cunt!

Gronya *slaps her.*

Carol   Ow! He's got Chinkie stuffed in his hat!

Gronya   Show me your helmet!

Gobbel   My – ?

Gronya   SHOW ME YOUR HELMET!

Quickly, he does. **Gronya** *snatches it and looks inside. Pause.*

There's nothing in here.

Carol   No, but it was, I promise! He must have got rid of it!

Gronya   Are you telling lies again, my girl?

Carol   No, I swear, on your life I'm not!

Gronya   Now, Carol – I want the truth now – I don't want any lies, you understand?

Carol   I'm not lying – !

Gronya   Shush, now – listen to me; did anybody touch you?

Carol   Touch me?

Gronya   You know what I mean; in a way they shouldn't have.

Pause.

Carol   Yes.

Blunt *and* **Gobbel** *are shocked.*

Blunt   Now just hold on a –

She shuts him up with a look.

Gronya   You – had best be very, very quiet.

He takes this on board.

Now don't lie about this, babe – this is very important – this is like a matter of life and death. Who was it that touched you – in a way they shouldn't have touched you?

Pause.

Carol? Who was it?

Carol   I told you. It was Uncle Bernie!

Gronya *slaps her on the head.*

Gronya   You rotten little liar!

Carol   I'm not – he did it again tonight!

Gronya   Don't you dare talk that way! Your uncle Bernie's not laid a finger on you!

Carol   How do you know?

Gronya   Cos he's my brother, that's why, and I know he'd never lay a finger on you!

Carol   He makes me play lollies!

Gronya   Right, that's it, you cunt! You get back to the house this minute and go straight to your bed or Santa'll be getting a knife in his belly! On you go, right now! Run!

Carol *exits.* **Gronya** *turns to face them.*

Gronya   What did you two freaks think you were going to do?! Feed my daughter to your pervert pal?!

Blunt   Now just – control yourself –

Gronya   I am controlling myself, mate! You'll know when I'm not controlling myself because I'll be splashing around in your pervert guts like a sugar-rush kid in a paddling pool!

Blunt   But we're not perverts, we're stripagrams!

Gronya   Bollocks!

Gobbel   It might be bollocks, but it's true!

Gronya   All right then. If you're stripagrams – strip!!

Pause.

Blunt   Strip?

Gronya   Show me your routine! Come on!

Blunt   We can't.

Gronya   Why not?

Blunt   Because we –

Gobbel   We forgot the music.

Blunt   That's right! After all that, we forgot to bring the music! Can you believe it?

Gronya   There's a tape in the machine.

Blunt   Not ours.

Gronya   If it's music, you can strip to it.

Blunt   You'd think so, wouldn't you, but actually it's not –

Gronya   Now, you listen to me, skinbag – I don't care if it's Stephen fucking Fry reading *Harry bumboy Potter*; you'll be stripping to it. Or I'll be stripping the flesh from your nonce-loving bones! Now get on with it!

Pause. They shuffle nervously forward.

All of you.

She nods at **Shandy**.

Blunt   Him?

Gronya   You're a team, aren't you?

Shandy   Did you know – that there are actually skidmarks on the Turin Shroud?

Blunt   But he's . . .

It's not going to wash. **Blunt** *and* **Gobbel** *hoist the vicar to his feet.* **Gronya** *picks up a remote control and points it at the stereo.*

Gronya   This had better be good.

She clicks on the tape. It's an instrumental version of 'The Windmills of Your Mind'.

Almost weeping, they begin their strip. This should be improvised for maximum comic effect. They strip to their underwear.

Finally, the track ends. Pause. **Gronya** *nods.*

Gronya   If you're stripagrams, I'm Princess fucking Stephanie! Prepare to be vandalised!

Suddenly, there's the sound of snarling. **Blunt** *screams and flips backwards over the couch.*

Gobbel   What's wrong?!

He surfaces, clutching at his helmet.

Blunt   It's alive!

Gobbel   What is?!

Blunt   What do you think?!

Gobbel   It can't be!
(*To* **Gronya**.) It's alive!

Gronya   What's alive?!

Pause.

Gobbel   Nothing.

Gronya   What d'you mean, nothing?

Again, **Blunt** *screams and twists around.*

Gronya   What's under that helmet?

Blunt   Nothing!

Gronya   We'll see about that!

She jumps on top of him, trying to get his helmet off.

Blunt   Help me!

Gobbel *jumps on too. The three of them roll around behind the sofa.* **Blunt** *manages to get free -* **Gobbel** *still grappling with* **Gronya**. **Blunt** *opens the window and tips the dog out of his helmet. It runs away.* **Gronya** *pulls him back down into the fray, which continues until . . . the phone starts ringing. Pause. The door opens and* **Garson** *comes in. She goes straight to it and picks it up.*

Garson   Hello?

(These italics heard only by her: 'Hello, Mum it's me. I'm really sorry the train got held up for hours at X but I'm on my way now.')

Right you are – so where are you now?

('I'm literally just minutes away, I'm in a taxi.')

Hearing this, **Blunt** *and* **Gobbel** *and* **Gronya** *stop fighting. They look up from behind the sofa.*

All right, dear.

('I'll be there any minute now.')

Sheepishly, **Balthasar** *pokes his head round the door.* **Garson** *signals him to come in.*

I'll put the kettle on, shall I?

('Oooh yes, I could do with a cup of tea, journey I've had.')

All right, dear. I daresay your father'll be there to meet you.

Balthasar *nods.*

('OK, bye!')

Garson   See you soon.

She puts the phone down.

Blunt *and* **Gobbel** *stand.*

Balthasar   I'm sorry, it was just the phone was –

Garson   Oh, don't be so wet! If you've all finished behaving like lunatics, perhaps we could have our living room back?

Blunt   Who was that?

Garson   Who was what?

Blunt   On the phone?

Balthasar   Oh, that was Carol – wasn't it?

Garson *nods.*

Blunt   Carol?

Gronya   Whose Carol?

Gobbel   Carol Carol?

Balthasar   No, our Carol –

Gronya   Your Carol?

Blunt   Carol Carol?

Gobbel   Both Carols?

Balthasar   No, just Carol.

Shandy   Carol, that was the name! She's the one that's dead!

Garson   She's not dead. She's just been on the train.

Balthasar   What happened to her car?

Garson   She doesn't have a car.

Balthasar   She does, doesn't she?

Garson   I told you; she sold it.

Balthasar   She sold it!

Garson   Oh, she was worried about that greenhouse thing – you know what she's like – so she sold it to some friend of hers –

Gobbel   She sold it?

Blunt   To a friend!

Balthasar   When was this?

Garson   Oh, about a week ago. Sold it to a friend for next to nothing. I told you all this.

Balthasar   Did you?

Garson   I said to her, wait till after Christmas and drive here because the trains are always busy and getting held up, but no, no; she knew better, and then what happens? She gets held up for four hours near Crewe.

Blunt   So where is she now?

Garson   She's just on her way in a taxi. Say's she'll be here in a few minutes. I'm going to put the kettle on.

Balthasar   Oh, yes, a cup of tea – would anyone care for . . . ?

Garson   Not them. When I return I shall expect you all to be gone, thank you.

She picks up a glass of water and throws it on **Shandy**, *who splutters into full consciousness.*

Shandy   What in the name of – ?!

Garson   That includes you . . . Reverend.

Garson *exits.*

Balthasar   I'm terribly sorry, it's been a long day for her and she can get a bit . . . short. She doesn't mean to be rude.

Gobbel *grabs* **Blunt**.

Gobbel   Blunt! She's alive! She's really alive this time! She is, isn't she?

Blunt   Looks like it.

Gobbel   They got it wrong, didn't they?! Like I said! It must've been her friend that died – but they could only identify her from the car wreck?!

Blunt (*nods*)   That must be it.

Gobbel   I'm so happy, Blunt!! I'm so happy!! We're saved! It's all worked out! We were right not to tell them! We're saved!!

He hugs **Blunt**.

Happy Christmas, Blunt!!

He hugs **Gronya**.

Happy Christmas, PAPS woman, even though you were going to put fish up our todgers and paddle in our guts!

He picks up a bunch of balloons and throws them in the air – taking two for himself. He then goes to **Balthasar** *and hugs him.*

And Bulbousarse! Especially you! Your life's not ruined after all! Happy Christmas!

Balthasar   Oh – my life's not – ? Well, thank you, and to you . . .

Next he goes to **Shandy** *and attempts to embrace him.*

Happy Christmas, Father Shandy!

Shandy   Get away from me, you madman!

Blunt   He's only trying to be friendly.

Shandy   Friendly? Do you realise what you've done, you two idiots?

Gobbel   What?

Shandy   I was meant to be on stage fifteen minutes ago!

Gronya   On stage in what?

Shandy   We're doing *Cabaret* at the church hall. It was a fund-raiser for Barbardo's! Well, if you think you've heard the end of this, any of you – !

Gobbel   Don't be like that, it's Christmas! Have a balloon!

Gobbel *gives him a balloon.*

Shandy   A balloon! I'll show you what I think of your damnable balloon!!

He bursts it, with a bang! Suddenly, **Balthasar** *clutches his chest and collapses.*

Gronya   Jesus!

Gronya *runs to him. The door opens and* **Garson** *comes in.*

Garson   What's happened?!

She sees **Balthasar** *on the floor.*

What the – ?!

Gronya *looks up at her, fingers on* **Balthasar***'s pulse, her face telling the story.*

Oh no – No, Balthasar!

She drops to her knees beside him.

Oh, darling – oh, my darling –

Pause. The door opens. It's **Carol** *– their daughter – laden with presents.*

Carol   HAPPY CHRISTMAS, EVERY – !

She stops in her tracks: sees her father, attended by **Garson**. *Sees the vicar in suspenders,* **Gronya**, **Blunt** *and* **Gobbel** *in their underwear. Pause.*

What's going on?

Beat.

Blunt/Gobbel   Your dad's dead.

Lights out.

By the same Author

Anthony Neilson Plays: One
The Censor
Stitching

Methuen Modern Plays

include work by

Jean Anouilh
John Arden
Margaretta D'Arcy
Peter Barnes
Sebastian Barry
Brendan Behan
Dermot Bolger
Edward Bond
Bertolt Brecht
Howard Brenton
Anthony Burgess
Simon Burke
Jim Cartwright
Caryl Churchill
Noël Coward
Lucinda Coxon
Sarah Daniels
Nick Darke
Nick Dear
Shelagh Delaney
David Edgar
David Eldridge
Dario Fo
Michael Frayn
John Godber
Paul Godfrey
David Greig
John Guare
Peter Handke
David Harrower
Jonathan Harvey
Iain Heggie
Declan Hughes
Terry Johnson
Sarah Kane
Charlotte Keatley
Barrie Keeffe
Howard Korder

Robert Lepage
Stephen Lowe
Doug Lucie
Martin McDonagh
John McGrath
Terrence McNally
David Mamet
Patrick Marber
Arthur Miller
Mtwa, Ngema & Simon
Tom Murphy
Phyllis Nagy
Peter Nichols
Joseph O'Connor
Joe Orton
Louise Page
Joe Penhall
Luigi Pirandello
Stephen Poliakoff
Franca Rame
Mark Ravenhill
Philip Ridley
Reginald Rose
David Rudkin
Willy Russell
Jean-Paul Sartre
Sam Shepard
Wole Soyinka
Shelagh Stephenson
C. P. Taylor
Theatre de Complicite
Theatre Workshop
Sue Townsend
Judy Upton
Timberlake Wertenbaker
Roy Williams
Victoria Wood

Methuen Contemporary Dramatists
include

Peter Barnes (three volumes)
Sebastian Barry
Edward Bond (six volumes)
Howard Brenton
   (two volumes)
Richard Cameron
Jim Cartwright
Caryl Churchill (two volumes)
Sarah Daniels (two volumes)
Nick Darke
David Edgar (three volumes)
Ben Elton
Dario Fo (two volumes)
Michael Frayn (two volumes)
Paul Godfrey
John Guare
Peter Handke
Jonathan Harvey
Declan Hughes
Terry Johnson (two volumes)
Bernard-Marie Koltès
David Lan
Bryony Lavery
Doug Lucie
David Mamet (three volumes)

Martin McDonagh
Duncan McLean
Anthony Minghella
   (two volumes)
Tom Murphy (four volumes)
Phyllis Nagy
Anthony Nielsen
Philip Osment
Louise Page
Joe Penhall
Stephen Poliakoff
   (three volumes)
Christina Reid
Philip Ridley
Willy Russell
Ntozake Shange
Sam Shepard (two volumes)
Wole Soyinka (two volumes)
David Storey (three volumes)
Sue Townsend
Michel Vinaver (two volumes)
Michael Wilcox
David Wood (two volumes)
Victoria Wood

Methuen World Classics

include

Jean Anouilh (two volumes)
John Arden (two volumes)
Arden & D'Arcy
Brendan Behan
Aphra Behn
Bertolt Brecht (six volumes)
Büchner
Bulgakov
Calderón
Čapek
Anton Chekhov
Noël Coward (seven volumes)
Eduardo De Filippo
Max Frisch
John Galsworthy
Gogol
Gorky
Harley Granville Barker
   (two volumes)
Henrik Ibsen (six volumes)
Lorca (three volumes)

Marivaux
Mustapha Matura
David Mercer (two volumes)
Arthur Miller (five volumes)
Molière
Musset
Peter Nichols (two volumes)
Clifford Odets
Joe Orton
A. W. Pinero
Luigi Pirandello
Terence Rattigan
   (two volumes)
W. Somerset Maugham
   (two volumes)
August Strindberg
   (three volumes)
J. M. Synge
Ramón del Valle-Inclán
Frank Wedekind
Oscar Wilde

For a complete catalogue of Methuen Drama titles
write to:

Methuen Drama
215 Vauxhall Bridge Road
London SW1V 1EJ

or you can visit our website at:

www.methuen.co.uk